From AAA to XXX:

A Dictionary/Commentary
on Porn and Porn Addiction

From AAA to XXX:

A Dictionary/Commentary on Porn and Porn Addiction

ALTERNATIVE TITLE:

Ladies and Porn Guys and Babes, O-Mi*! (Oh My!)

(Chant to the rhythm of "Lions and Tigers and Bears, Oh My!" From The Wizard of Oz)

Olivia Luv

Published by Future Directions Publishing

ISBN 979-8-9850626-0-1 (paperback)
ISBN 979-8-9850626-1-8 (eBook)

Printed in the United States of America

Contents

Contents

Contents

*O-Mi (pronounced Oh My! with eyes popping)

Ogle-Masturbatory Image. "Porn" has no agreed-upon definition, so this is a useful acronym, which includes two activities
that are typically part of porn use, "**ogle**" and "masturbation."
The term is broad enough to cover everything from the _**Sports
Illustrated Swimsuit**_ images that many (probably more men
than women) argue "are not porn" to the hardest core, most
brutal films on **Pornhub.com**. Though these images are highly
variable, they are all about escape, titillation, and for those who
have **romantic** partners, **mental infidelity**.

Introduction

People who view pornography are doing something that many of them consider unhealthy, and some of them cannot stop. A majority of the population thinks that porn is immoral. That includes many porn users. Porn is now being recognized in many places as a **public health** hazard. It damages users, their partners, and the sex performers who participate in it. The aim of this dictionary and commentary is to help anyone who wants to rethink porn. This may include people in all three of the aforementioned categories. If even a few readers come to fresh insights or understandings or begin to use new terminology or an old term in a novel way, the dictionary will have served its purpose. It is also important to note at the outset that the underlying **values** of this dictionary and commentary are health and happiness. I believe that these values are shared by almost everyone, even when they have lost sight of them momentarily.

The list of terms included below is not exhaustive; that would be a much larger undertaking. Instead, it is focused on some essential terms that porn users, their romantic partners, online sex actors, and therapists should know and on ideas that

1

may lead to thinking about porn in a new way. It may also be useful to researchers since it contains hypotheses about what might be examined in future studies. An underlined, bolded term within the text indicates a term (or a derivative of a term) that is defined and discussed elsewhere in the document. It will only be bolded and underlined the first time it appears in the discussion of a particular term to enhance readability (but it will be bolded and underlined again when it first appears in discussions of other terms). Additional terms are bolded for emphasis but are not in the list of defined terms and hence are not underlined. Some of the terms are new and have been coined for this document or are terms not often associated with porn or porn **addiction**. In those cases, the reader will be led to an entry by hyperlinks (electronic version only) found in other parts of the book. The word "porn" is never bolded in this document because it is never defined (there is no agreed-upon definition). The term **O-Mi** is only bolded and underlined in this introduction. Familiarity with its meaning is assumed in the rest of the document.

The terms, except for the first (O-Mi, on p. 1) and the last (**solutions** in the conclusion), will be in alphabetical order (**AAA** to **XXX**). O-Mi is a new term introduced as an alternative to "porn." It is an acronym. The letters that make up the acronym represent two activities that are part of online sex viewing—and, of course, sex magazine and film viewing that are not online. By citing these two activities (ogling and masturbation) in the term itself, there is more clarity than in the word "porn." Note, however, that the term "porn," though not defined in this document, will be used frequently because it is familiar to readers and because it is used by many of the cited sources. For these reasons, using it will enhance the readability of the book, but it is hoped that readers will see the utility of the acronym O-Mi for future use in discussions of sexual images.

Thus, "O-Mi" will often be used here with the word "porn" but will sometimes be used alone.

Also, note that in many, but not all, instances no differentiation will be made between a porn user and a porn addict. Obviously, not all users are addicts; some users do not have the level of **compulsion** and the sense of losing control while viewing O-Mi images that addicts have. But negative effects on the brain occur without addiction (Love et al., 2015; *Watching Pornography Rewires the Brain*, 2019; Wilson, 2017, p. 107), and it is hard to pinpoint when porn use becomes an addiction. The outcomes for the O-Mi viewer are often more of a matter of degree than of type (except for the minority of child porn viewers who are pursued by law enforcement). Hence, no attempt is made here to draw a hard and fast line between porn use and addiction.

So, let's look at **AAA** to **XXX** and a lot in between. I'll examine our current porn conundrum and explore new and old ways of thinking about porn. Since many of the entries and commentary examine reasons why porn use is problematic, the conclusion will lay out some remedies to the tsunami of porn use.

Terms and Commentary

AAA: accessibility, anonymity, and affordability

The Triple A Engine of Porn. They are the three reasons why porn is so ubiquitous and tempting in the electronics age.

Porn is readily accessible on electronic devices of all types (with most use occurring on phones and tablets, not computers). In many cases, the user is completely anonymous; no one knows about their O-Mi viewing. With the internet, users need pay no money, unlike users in the past who bought magazines and videos and were perhaps more likely to go to strip clubs to get their fill of nudity and semi-nudity. As a consequence of AAA, there is an explosion of porn and, with it, a pandemic of use and **addiction** (de Alarcón et al., 2019; Cooper & Scherer, 1999) (see **porn pandemic**).

Accountability partner

A person who helps another stop a problematic habit or **addiction**. In this book, an accountability partner is someone who helps a porn user or addict stop viewing O-Mi's.

The accountability partner keeps abreast (pun intended) of the actions of the person who is trying to change and calls them on it when they backslide. They can be a professional (perhaps a therapist or health-care worker), a fellow **twelve-step** member, a friend, a **romantic** partner, or spouse. They know the porn user and his O-Mi viewing habits well and help address the anonymity issue of porn (see **accessibility, anonymity, and affordability**).

Many people will not be able to get off porn without an accountability partner. For an accountability partner to be helpful, however, the porn user must commit to being open and calm when asked about his progress. Of course, some accountability partners are unreliable and don't take their responsibilities seriously. If you are trying to kick a porn habit or an addiction, don't delay in finding a different accountability partner if your current one is not helping you stop using porn.

Addiction

Repetitive behaviors resulting from a craving for some stimulus. More and more of the stimulus is required to get the "high." Over time, the circuitry of the brain is rewired.

With regard to O-Mi usage, changes in brain structure begin to occur with even small amounts of viewing. One study showed that 16 percent of high school seniors (an age group where sexual appetites would normally be high) who consumed porn *once a week* experienced low sexual desire (compared to zero percent of abstainers) (Wilson, 2017, p. 52).

All addictions are diseases of the brain. Once the brain is altered, people make consistently poor choices around the substance or behavior to which they are addicted (Smith, 2019). Since all addictions involve similar brain changes, this book will reference research on other addictions that suggest hypotheses about porn addiction (which has not reached the same level of research). **Smoking**, in particular, is frequently compared to porn consumption, but findings on other addictions such as alcoholism and heroin dependency are cited because they may also suggest insights about what we should examine in future studies of porn use.

Addictions increasingly take over people's lives, crowding out other activities and **relationships**. Some people will remain casual and occasional viewers of O-Mi's, but **accessibility, affordability, and anonymity**, along with loneliness, depression, boredom, and horniness, may result in pornography addiction (see **chipping**, **compulsion**, **defenses, psychological**, **Dr. Jekyll and Mr. Hyde**, **mental health**, and **pornaholic**).

The DSM (Diagnostic and Statistical Manual of Mental Disorders) does not recognize porn addiction as an illness. However, the World Health Organization diagnostic manual (the International Classification of Diseases, or ICD-11) has added compulsive sexual disorder to its roster of diagnoses. Its definition appears to encompass porn addictions (Silverstein, 2018).

BDSM

Bondage, dominance/discipline, sadism/submission, and masochism. These acts are commonly depicted on internet sex sites.

These acts are referred to as "**kink**" by those who are positive toward them or as "**sexual deviance**" by those who are concerned about mixing power, aggression, and violence (whether "role-playing" or real) with sex. BDSM is on a continuum with bondage (women in porn are often tied up or handcuffed) on one end of the scale and sadism and masochism on the other end. Many porn viewers seek out BDSM online and then want to try it themselves and get partners involved.

Though BDSM activity is widespread in the online sex world, the only random sample study conducted on it to date was in Australia in 2001-2002. That study found that 1.8 percent of people had been active in BDSM activities in the prior year, and these practices were more common among gay, lesbian, and bisexual people than among heterosexuals (Richters et al., 2008). Given the stigma associated with the subject, there was probably some underreporting in the study. Nonetheless, the number of people who participate in BDSM activities regularly appears to be very low.

Porn is likely making BDSM more acceptable, but do we really want general cultural acceptance of sex that mixes the enactment of power disparities, gender roles (men are usually in the dominant position and women are usually, but not always, in a submissive position), and role-playing or real aggression and violence, even if it is consensual? (In online depictions, BDSM is not always consensual—see **trafficking** and **violence against women**) (see also **gender inequality**, **hard-core**, **mental health**, **Pornhub.com**, **racial inequality**, and **XXX**).

Beautiful women

Lovely ladies and sexy babes. These are only two of many synonyms that porn users put into their search engines when looking for O-Mi's.

Many of the women in the online sex world look great, but they are so surgically and otherwise altered that it would be hard to identify their "before" appearance with the "after" photos and films available for O-Mi consumption (see **cyborg femmes**).

What Hugh Hefner's "playmates" in the Playboy Mansion did to their appearance suggests some of the ways that many online sex performers alter their bodies for porn users. In the 21st century Mansion, all of the playmates and bunnies had breast implants, and most of them had **nose jobs**. They bleached their hair blonde. Aging was so verboten for the playmates that many of them began to use botox in their early 20s. As one of them said in her book, she wasn't born "beautiful," she made herself "beautiful." I write "beautiful" in quotation marks because what is seen as beautiful varies from era to era and society to society; the porn world is now having a significant impact on views of what women must do to themselves to be considered beautiful (Madison, 2015).

The ubiquity of plastic surgery among women who work in the O-Mi industry indicates that the plastic surgery and porn industries are heavily intertwined. Part of the reason that the images are so addicting is that the women are implausibly perfect—most of them have undergone plastic surgeries and are airbrushed and photoshopped to boot. Thus, we can ask: Are porn users admiring beautiful women or skillful plastic surgery and digital fakery? And how many real women could hope to compete with such unreal images?

Big porn

The porn industry, which is enormous in terms of the amount of viewing done online and the large dollar figures earned by porn purveyors.

The porn industry uses tactics analogous to those of the tobacco industry (which has sometimes been called Big Tobacco) to protect its bottom line. The porn industry does not want the public to be aware of the negative effects of porn. It wants a glamourous, "cool" image, just as the tobacco companies did in their heyday. But in the end, **smoking** was recognized as a **public health** hazard, and smoking rates decreased substantially.

O-Mi's are likely to meet the same fate (*Does the Porn Industry Use "Tobacco Industry Tactics," 2018*; Eberstadt, 2009).

Bottom feeder films and TV programs

Films or TV programs showing gratuitous semi-nudity, nudity, and sexual activity, which add little to the plot but exist largely to titillate their audience and increase sales. Besides offering titillation, they often make the abnormal and uncommon appear normal. They may undercut social norms like those against incest and **violence against women**. These movies and tv shows usually have few if any redeeming **values.**

It is important to note that my comments pertain to porn users who want to break their porn habits. Upon seeing titillating scenes and nudity, they may seek another movie with the actress or actresses in a greater state of undress or in more prurient scenes. Or they may head for their computer or other electronic devices and google an actress's name and the word "nude." In contrast, other people can "take it or leave it." They can see gratuitous sex and nudity and respond with moderate interest, indifference, or perhaps disgust. The material is not hugely enticing. Many people will have some exposure to bottom-feeder films and TV programs, but these media do not **trigger** a search for more explicit material. However, someone trying to end a porn habit needs to avoid these programs to not endanger their **recovery**.

All **XXX** and most NC-17 movies can be categorized as bottom-feeder films. (Some NC-17 films have a degree of artistic merit, but many do not and are **soft-core** vehicles for titillation.) Again, the remarks here pertain to people with significant porn habits. If they want to end their O-Mi habit, they should make sure that these films are blocked on their television and other devices.

It is important to discuss NR (not rated) films as well. Films have no rating for a variety of reasons. They might, for example, be a nonfiction documentary. But many films have NR labels because the producers do not want an NC-17 rating; many theaters will not show NC-17 movies. Thus, NR films are often, but not always, bottom-feeder films and sexually focused. It is a good idea to block these films as well.

Smart TVs constitute a special challenge. They are beyond the reach of **porn blockers** that work simultaneously for computers, smartphones, and tablets. Even if the TV is in "the family room," they are a hazard to recovering porn users when no one is home or when family members are busy with activities in other areas of the house or apartment. The most effective way to deal with this problem is by blocking porn via the household router (*Block Porn at Home on Your Wifi*, n.d.) This is the preferred first step in dealing with all online porn because it blocks it from every electronic device that uses that router. Further protection can then be added through porn blockers like Covenant Eyes or Net Nanny.

Some (but certainly not all) R movies are bottom-feeder films. They often contain sexual abuse and **BDSM**. Some movie services, particularly Amazon and Netflix, are known for including nudity and sex, which add little to the storyline of their productions but will earn them a rating that might attract a greater audience and increased profits (Strand, 2021).

Some R movies are excellent. Almost no one would want to block the whole category. It is possible to selectively block sex scenes, violence, and profanity (see VidAngel.com). A porn user triggered by these films no longer needs to rely solely on **willpower**, which is notoriously poor at preventing slips or full **relapse**.

Some but not all TV-MA (TV for mature audiences) shows also fit the bottom-feeder designation. As is true for films, it is possible to use VidAngel to selectively block sexually provocative scenes, which might be problematic for recovering porn addicts.

Hotels are also a challenge for porn addicts (Smith, 2019, p.5). The recovering porn user should stay at hotels that do not offer porn channels. He or his partner should complain to hotel management when a hotel does offer these channels.

An O-Mi viewer who is trying to move away from his porn habit may **substitute** milder bottom-feeder films and programs for more explicit pornography. This may indicate progress, though not the reconnection with deeper values that is indicative of recovery (Amen & Smith, 2010, pp. 84, 85, 94; Peele, 2015).

Boycott

Refusal to buy from or otherwise support certain companies, people, or organizations in order to protest their actions or views.

Boycotts are a potential strategy for cutting into the profits of porn sites and the companies that advertise on them. As **Pornhub.com** and other O-Mi sites seek to expand their pool of mainstream advertisers, boycotts of companies that choose to advertise on these sites are likely to follow (Taube, 2013) (see **solutions** in the conclusion).

Brain damage

Brain injury, which **neuroscience** is now able to investigate and evaluate.

There is some debate about whether the brain differences seen in porn users are a cause or consequence of O-Mi viewing (Hess, n.d.); however, case histories suggest that it is more likely a cause of brain damage than a simple correlation (Wilson, 2017, p. 28). Porn use, like alcoholism, appears to be an organic insult to the brain (Vaillant, 2012, p. 180). It may reverse the normal process of brain development and leave the porn user in a perpetual state of immaturity (*Watching Pornography Rewires the Brain*, 2019). The amount of O-Mi viewing required to damage the brain is small, and measurable impacts on the brain occur even when a user is not addicted (Wilson, 2017, p. 107).

Here are some of the brain differences found in men who view a significant amount of porn versus men who don't: There is erosion of the prefrontal cortex, smaller amounts of gray matter, lower ability to focus, and less impulse control. Some studies also suggest that O-Mi viewing causes brain fog and a decline in short term memory. Men with a porn habit are more likely to be depressed (*Watching Pornography Rewires the Brain*, 2019).

Brain scans of porn addicts are sometimes shown to their **romantic** partner so that they can see that the O-Mi viewer has developed a physical and not just psychological problem. This may lead to greater sympathy for the O-Mi addict (Smith, 2019, p. 7).

Cheating

Unfaithfulness to one's **romantic** partner.

A significant proportion of the partners of porn users consider porn to be cheating. So do some of the users themselves. Porn leads to fantasies of sex with women who are not one's partner, which is possible even if a male has **erectile dysfunction** (which some research suggests can be caused by porn use (see **PIED** below). In most men, it leads to masturbation to the sexual images, which frequently means less sex with their mates and the intrusion of O-Mi images into their minds during sex with their partner. Desire for his partner typically decreases, and sex with her may also begin to seem increasingly unsatisfactory compared to what he sees online, as may his lover's body, leading to a downward spiral in the quantity and quality of sex with his girlfriend or wife (Paul, 2005, Ch. 5). Porn users, including those who are **chipping**, are, by definition, *mentally* unfaithful (see **mental infidelity**), and research suggests that porn leads many to be **physical cheaters** as well.

Even many women who do not consider porn to be cheating are uneasy with their partner's O-Mi viewing, including young women who have grown up during the **porn pandemic** (Pappas, 2012). Regnerus and Uecker (2011, p. 96) note that some young women tolerate porn because "to protest it would be to appear reactionary or anachronistic, both of which most people prefer to avoid." They also suggest that women are increasingly likely to find that young men are unwilling to commit to **relationships** (p. 99), an idea which is born out by the developing literature on **sex recession**. Some men like porn so much that it is more attractive to them than sex with real women.

As the **addictive** nature of porn comes to be known, the uneasiness of partners is likely to increase. Pascal-Emmanuel Gobry (2019) puts it this way: "[G]iven what porn addiction does to male sexuality, from the female perspective, sex with a porn addict sounds like an experiment you don't want to repeat." Romantic partners who feel betrayed by their porn using partner can seek help from **twelve-step** groups like **Infidelity Survivors Anonymous (ISA)**.

Chick repellent

Porn.

It is true that an increasing number of women, especially young women, look at porn. It is no longer strictly a male domain and most likely never has been. It is also true that many people, especially women, find porn abhorrent. That doesn't mean that their bodies won't respond to seeing O-Mi's. It does mean that porn conflicts with their **identity**, **values**, and what they want for their lives.

The women who use porn are disproportionately likely to have been exposed to it as children or sexually abused in other ways (Kasl, 1989, pp. 268–269), but the porn industry is working hard to increase the number of female viewers. As a result, childhood exposure to porn or past sexual abuse is probably less associated with women's O-Mi viewing now than in the past (Eberstadt, 2009). Men also encourage women to view porn as a way to get them to participate in sexual activities that they would not otherwise consider (Paul, 2005).

Chipping

Viewing porn occasionally and recreationally but not at a level that most people would consider **addiction**.

This occasional use is analogous to chipping by heroin users (see **drugs**). For those who see porn as **mental infidelity**, chipping is still **cheating**, but more like the occasional one-night-stand or a quickie with someone from a hook-up app rather than a full-blown affair. **Romantic** partners who feel betrayed by their porn-using partner, including a partner who is chipping, can seek help from **twelve-step** groups like **Infidelity Survivors Anonymous (ISA)**.

Compulsion

The irresistible urge to engage in an activity, an obsession.

An addict will perform an act repeatedly to avoid negative emotions such as severe porn cravings and anxiety or physical symptoms indicating withdrawal, such as jitters, sweating, tears, headaches, and insomnia (Wilson, 2017, pp. 134–137). Porn use can become a persistent, nonvoluntary activity, sometimes done almost in a trance (Carnes, 1983, p. 10).[1] Compulsions are not easily cast aside. This nonvoluntary viewing may not be particularly **pleasurable** but is used to deal with stress, loneliness, depression, and past trauma (see **defenses, psychological**). Thus, porn use is not necessarily **fun**, though the jokes surrounding it assume that it is fun (see **addiction**, **pain**, and **suffering**).

Coolidge effect

The re-arousal exhibited in males (and to a lesser extent in females) when a new sexual partner becomes available, accompanied by a decline in interest in a current sexual partner.

It has been demonstrated that in a variety of mammalian species erections occur more quickly after sex if there is a new female available for mating. It is sometimes used to explain men's interest in porn and their often rapid clicking from one pornographic image to the next (Hughes et al., 2020) (see **evolutionary theory**). The theory got its name from a story about President Coolidge. Coolidge's wife, when visiting a farm and seeing many hens but only one rooster, asked how many times a day the rooster was able to copulate. The reply was "dozens of times each day." She said, "Tell that to President Coolidge." When the president stopped by the hen house later, he was told about the frequency of the rooster's sexual performance. He then asked if it was always with the same hen and was told that it was a different hen every time. He replied, "Tell that to Mrs. Coolidge."

However, the rooster in the henhouse lives in a highly artificial situation, and the animal experiments used to test this theory occur in human-made laboratories. Most bird species are monogamous (Breed & Moore, 2015, pp. 357–393). Although they currently exist only in environs that humans create for

---

1 A revised 2001 edition of Pat Carnes's book *Out of the Shadows: Understanding Sex Addiction* is also available.

them, chickens are descended mostly from jungle fowl, who appear to be monogamous in normal circumstances (Britannica, 2019).

The online porn **environment** is even more artificial than the one faced by the rooster in the hen house. One male views the images of many women who are **cyborg femmes** (often very different than their natural, real-life appearance). He does not mate *with* them but merely clicks from one image to the next and *imagines* that he is mating with some of them. These situations do not represent the evolutionary situations of humans or other mammals, and the long-term **reproductive success** of humans can be undermined by the disinterest in **relationships** that porn creates (see **intercourse** and **sex recession**).

Humans, like most bird species, many primates, and prairie voles, might be more wired for monogamy than promiscuity, whether enacted in real life or online (Hassed, 2017). The Coolidge effect might be greatly diminished by learning good relationship skills and forming an **oxytocin**-based relationship. (Love, 2016)

Cyborg

An organism which combines biological and technological components.

Humans with artificial heart valves, cochlear implants and, pertinent to this dictionary, breast implants fit this definition of cyborg.[2] Though some O-Mi viewers idealize internet sex performers as almost perfect "beauties," the majority are cyborgs, just as the Terminator (played by Arnold Schwarzenegger in The Terminator franchise) is a cyborg who combines technological

---

2 See, for example, "China's 'Sexy Cyborg' Took on Silicon Valley's Bro Culture—and Won," by Jessica Meyers, *Los Angeles Times*, Dec. 7, 2017, https://www.latimes.com/world/asia/la-fg-china-sexy-cyborg-2017-story.html.

and human components. Most O-Mi's have fake breasts, and many have undergone other plastic surgery. These surgeries have health risks (Grudzen et al., 2009), but for many online models and sex performers, these nonhuman alterations are necessary for them to participate in their line of work and make a living. References to **"bionic boobs"** are recognitions that the viewer is not looking at natural beauty but at someone who is partly a surgical creation (for more, see **cyborg femmes**, **female breast mutilation**, **female genital mutilation**, **nose jobs**, and **sexy vs. sexual**).

Cyborg femmes

A term applying to women who have incorporated artificial parts into their bodies with the specific intent to appear more womanly. The most common artificial parts seen in the online sex world are breast implants (see **beautiful women**, **female breast mutilation**, and **sexy vs. sexual**).

Defenses, psychological

Unconscious mechanisms aimed at reducing anxiety and psychological pain. The term suggests that there are elements of porn use that are beyond the realm of conscious reflection.

Use of porn is an immature defense mechanism against boredom, loneliness, and past trauma. Fantasy, as it relates to porn use, is also an unconscious defense mechanism (Stansvik, 2018). Mature defense mechanisms include humor, sublimation, altruism, and suppression (Vaillant, 2012, p. 268).

An immature defense mechanism (such as porn) can be outgrown. The user or addict needs to address the underlying causes of **addiction** through **therapy** or other means and find a healthy, supportive **environment** that encourages them to become **porn-free** and evolve toward a nonexploitive sexuality (see **maturing out**, **mental health**, and **recovery**).

Denial

The view that O-Mi **addiction** is not real, and if it is, it is not what the porn addict is experiencing.

Porn addicts are generally in denial early in their addiction, but denial can also reoccur periodically as the porn user tries to end his porn habit. If he is viewing less porn or viewing sporadically, the addict may claim that he no longer has an addiction. The nature of addiction, however, is that it gets rekindled easily. Just as going "on the wagon" is more often evidence of alcoholism than of **recovery** (Vaillant, 2012, p. 312), the "on the wagon" **pornaholic** may not be recovered and remains in danger of **relapse**.

If porn addiction turns out to be similar to **smoking** and alcohol addictions, it may take five years of abstinence for remission to be considered reliably secure (Vaillant, 2012, p. 308). And if porn addiction is like smoking and alcoholism, the addict will not be able to safely return to **chipping** behaviors but will need to stay consistently **porn-free**. There are many tools that can help them do this (see **accountability partner**, **porn blockers**, **relapse**, **solutions** in the conclusion, **stinking thinking**, **therapy**, and **twelve-step programs**).

The porn addict is usually in denial about the harm he does to others, including his children and **romantic** partner, who might be aware of his O-Mi viewing and the saved pictures and films on his computer and other electronic devices. And most porn users rarely, if ever, think about the damage done to women who perform sex online, who, for the most part, are not well paid, have no benefits, and may suffer both physical and psychological injury. On the contrary, porn viewers may think of porn workers as highly sexed and happy exhibitionists who want to show their all to thousands of men, but the reality is far more complicated than that (see **legal**, **mental health**, **pain**, **shorter lives**, **suffering**, **trafficked**, and **virtual prostitutes**).

Denial also exists on the societal level. Many deny that porn addiction is real. This is accompanied by beliefs that the O-Mi viewer is always and only having **fun**, that porn use cannot and will not damage the user's personal life, and that **compulsion** does not drive the porn addict to their online viewing of sex images (Hatch, 2015) (see **divorce**, **erectile dysfunction**, **PIED**, and **shorter lives**).

Divorce

The legal termination of a marriage.

Porn use frequently causes marital breakups. Divorce lawyers say that well over half of divorces have porn as one of the causes, and sometimes it is the main cause. Viewing O-Mi's often leads to sex becoming less frequent or nonexistent (even in cases of "low" usage) in the O-Mi viewer's **relationship** with a partner (see **love** and **sex recession**). The addict may also abdicate other family responsibilities, such as taking care of their children. Some addicts use porn so heavily that they lose their jobs, which of course, may also be a factor in divorce. (Perry & Schleifer, 2018).

The divorces caused by porn as well as the **trauma** experienced by **romantic** partners of porn users and online sex performers are three of the many reasons that O-Mi viewing and porn **addiction** are serious **public health** concerns (see **chick repellent**, **erectile dysfunction**, **mental health**, **PIED**, and **shorter lives**).

Dopamine

A neurochemical often referred to as "the **pleasure** hormone" and "the craving neurochemical."

Dopamine is released by the hypothalamus and "causes you to want, desire, seek out and search" (Psychology Today Staff, n.d.). As Gary Wilson (2017, p. 75) explained it, "the message of dopamine isn't satisfaction. It's keep going, satisfaction is j-u-s-t around the corner." Consequently, many porn viewers engage in **edging**. They click on image after image, come close to orgasm, then stop and view more sexual images. Therefore, dopamine levels stay high throughout the experience.

With internet porn, it is possible to keep dopamine levels high for much longer than is healthy. When craving becomes frequent and O-Mi viewing is **compulsive**, the user has become addicted to the experience (but not to the dopamine itself). It takes a porn addict an average of 18 months to heal the damage to their dopamine receptors (Maltz & Maltz, 2008, p.20). Very high dopamine levels also block "falling in love" mechanisms and attachment (Blythe, n.d.).

Other neurochemicals released during O-Mi viewing include **oxytocin** and serotonin. The release of multiple chemicals suggests that it is more accurate to refer to the experience as a "neurochemical high" rather than a "dopamine hit."

Dr. Jekyll and Mr. Hyde

A person marked by having two sides to their personality, one good and one bad (Carnes, 1991, p. 229).

In the book by the same name, Dr. Jekyll, a respected middle-aged doctor, creates a potion that allows him to turn into Mr. Hyde, a young, pale, dwarfish version of himself who has no conscience and who seeks pleasures that are "monstrous" (Stevenson, 1886/1968, p. 91). Dr. Jekyll is kindly and well-liked;

his alternate self inspires revulsion. The two selves struggle with each other, but in the end, the pull of Mr. Hyde is too strong, and only the Hyde persona remains. Similarly, porn **addiction** (Mr. Hyde) can consume more and more hours. Over time, Dr. Jekyll, the better self, inhabits less and less of the addict's life.

"Nice guys" often use porn and compartmentalize their views of themselves so that their O-Mi use is not part of their self-image. Therefore, we see nice guy Dr. Jekyll on one side and porn user or addict Mr. Hyde on the other side. Hiding is key to porn viewing. Mr. Hyde hides not only from others but also from himself since he is usually in **denial** about the amount of time he spends with porn and the effects of his viewing on himself and other people. This denial is critical since most people, including many O-Mi users, value fidelity and **love** (Griffin-Shelley et al., 1995).

In Stevenson's book, Mr. Hyde lacked a conscience, and the conscience of an addict is somewhat to severely impaired. In an interview by Travis Smith, Dr. Patrick Carnes, a well-known expert on sex addiction, says it is critical for recovering porn viewers to regain their conscience. "Development of a moral compass" is essential to **recovery** but usually occurs late in the process (Smith, 2019, p. 4).

One could also say that purveyors of porn are cases of Dr. Jekyll and Mr. Hyde. The industry publicizes its involvement in humane causes such as "Clean the Beach," "Save Pandas, Make Porn," and anti-domestic abuse initiatives, all while contributing to addiction and other **mental health** problems, **divorce**, human **trafficking**, and other maladies (*5 Spooky Facts About Porn*, 2020). These positive contributions are supposed to hide pornography's Mr. Hyde (see **Big porn** and **public health**).

Drugs

Something that causes habituation or **addiction**. The term is usually used in reference to chemical substances, but it also refers to porn.

Working in the porn industry is abhorrent in many ways; in order to do it, many in the business abuse substances like alcohol and heroin (Grudzen et al., 2009). Some will develop addictions. Some will even die (see **shorter lives**). Even Hugh Hefner's "playmates" were often on drugs. Hefner encouraged "thigh opener" drugs, but some of the women living at the Playboy Mansion were on other drugs as well. Being a "girlfriend" of Hefner was a comfortable gig in some ways, and many of the women took drugs as part of the "glamorous" lifestyle they were leading. However, others appeared to use drugs to help them endure the interpersonal tensions that ran rampant through the Playboy Mansion and the emotional abuse and boredom that were part of being a bunny (Madison, 2015, p. 94; St. James, 2006).

Many women cannot perform sexually online without drugs. One male actor said about the female performers, "If they were completely sober, no alcohol, no drugs, I guarantee you most of them would probably have mental breakdowns" (Grudzen et al., 2009).

As noted above, porn itself acts like a drug. Both drugs and porn cause a neurochemical rush. Like drugs, porn is addicting. Consequently, porn is being called "the new drug" (see https://fightthenewdrug.org/). Porn is also referred to as **visual heroin** and **visual cocaine** (see **chipping**). The number of users and addicts suggests that the porn industry (see **Big porn**) is the biggest drug **pusher** in the world (Bennett, 2013).

Dupe

Someone who is being deceived or tricked. The **romantic** partner of a porn user may fit this label.

They may not know that their boyfriend or husband is viewing O-Mi's or, if they do, may feel helpless to stop it. O-Mi viewers usually hide their habits from their partners, except, perhaps, in cases where their partner has their own porn habit. (The user might, however, swap pictures with their friends.)

Lying is typically a part of **addiction** (Maltz & Maltz, 2008; Paul, 2005). Even O-Mi users who fall short of addiction understand that a significant part of society does not approve of their habit. The duplicity of porn users may make their partners feel like dupes.

For those who want to become **porn-free**, truth-telling will be an important part of their **recovery** and will increase their **intimacy** with their girlfriend or wife if they have one. The relationship will become more romantic and **loving**. "When the recovering porn user is honest and committed to healing, it is much more likely that his partner will be able to handle setbacks and continue to work together on mending the **relationship**" (Maltz & Maltz, 2008, p. 212). Foster and Hicks (2008, p. 202) say that truth-telling is a "critically important element in the creation of vigorous interpersonal relationships and (also) entire communities." It is also associated with better personal health (Foster et al., 2008), which will benefit the recovering porn user and everyone in his circle and (probably) a broader network of people beyond his immediate contacts (Christakis & Fowler, 2009, p. 116).

One sign that the porn user is lying is an insistence that his romantic partner **trust** him, regardless of the evidence. It would not occur to someone who is consistently honest to insist on trust; they would assume that their truth-telling is obvious (see

Dr. Jekyll and Mr. Hyde). Thus, the effort to make a girlfriend or wife into a dupe may include this insistence on trust.

Edging

Prolonging masturbation and delaying orgasm as a way to enhance sexual enjoyment.

O-Mi viewers often click on image after image, keeping **dopamine** levels high but avoiding orgasm for hours. This is pleasurable but can cause damage to the neurological system when done regularly. Dopamine receptors can take up to 18 months to heal after porn viewing is discontinued (see **brain damage** and **neuroscience**). Edging is an example of the seeking system in humans, which is more important to human survival than the satiation system (Wilson, 2017, p. 68). Edging involves constant seeking without release.

Enabling

Allowing and even encouraging someone to act in a way that is bad for them; therefore, helping the bad habit or **addiction** rather than the person.

Girlfriends and wives who do not want porn to be a part of their **relationship** should not help or encourage the user's O-Mi habit in any way (see **tough love**). It is not possible to stop someone from using if they are not ready to do so, but the partner should not do anything that helps the user or addict continue or increase their habit.

Entitlement

The feeling that one has the right to a particular privilege.

Some entitlements are granted by culture or law; others are

not recognized by the majority of people in the society but only by a particular subgroup. While not everyone thinks that porn is an entitlement, O-Mi users often feel that they have the prerogative to view any online sexual image. However, many porn users' real-life partners do not agree that their mate is entitled to use porn. Partners usually feel entitled in a very different way: they feel they have a right to the porn user's sexual focus and attention. Most don't want a partner whose sexuality is scattered around the internet and who has sex with hundreds or thousands of women in his imagination. The broader culture (of which both porn and non-porn users are still aware) largely supports the entitlement felt by the partners of O-Mi viewers.

Environment

The surroundings and circumstances in which a porn user or addict lives and the norms and expectations of their communities.

The environment has a huge impact on the degree of O-Mi viewing and might even stop a user in their tracks (see **solutions** in the conclusion). Since porn and **drug** use are often compared, the following quote regarding drug users returning from Vietnam and resolving their drug **addictions** might be instructive. (References to drugs have been changed to references to porn in the following passage.)

> You'd want to surround the porn addicts with people who love and care about them and who treat them as the **porn-free** persons they once were. You'd give them interesting work to do—perhaps designing posters for music bands of a type of music they love—so their minds would be distracted from the joys of porn. You'd create well publicized sanctions against porn use. You'd keep the porn economy underground, making the porn users have to sneak around

to obtain and use porn. You'd make sure their girlfriends and wives gave them a hard time about their porn use. You'd set up social taboos so that the addicts would feel derelict, even pathetic, if they kept using. You'd remove the contagious porn-using behavior from the environment—no more porn addicts around—and replace it with contagious porn-free behavior. And you would provide rich environmental cues— sights, songs, food, clothes, and homes—that remind the former addicts of their earlier porn-free **identities** (Heath & Heath, 2010, pp. 206–207).

Erectile dysfunction (ED)

Problems with getting and maintaining erections during sexual interactions. Ejaculation that is overly delayed and the inability to orgasm can also be aspects of erectile dysfunction.

The severity of dysfunction varies, and porn use might or might not be a contributing cause. However, one clue that porn is a cause is when a man can get erections with porn but not with real-life partners. The statistics are alarming. "Since the Kinsey report in the 1940s, studies have found roughly the same, stable rates of chronic ED: less than 1 percent among men younger than 30, less than 3 percent in men aged 30-45" (Gobry, 2019). But studies published since 2010 indicate a huge rise in ED, with rates among men under 40 ranging from 14 to 37 percent (Gobry, 2019). This is an increase of a large magnitude.

O-Mi viewers and their partners need to be aware that this is a possible side effect of porn use. In the past, erectile dysfunction was considered to be a problem mostly of older men. It is now also a young man's problem[3] (see **fear of aging**, **pornified**, and **PIED**).

---

3 See Martin Daubney's article "Men's Lives Are Being Ruined by Pornography. So Why Aren't We Angry About It?" The Telegraph, March 29, 2017. https://www.telegraph. co.uk/men/thinking-man/mens-lives-ruined-pornography-arent-angry/. The article summarizes the major findings of "Pornography Consumption and Satisfaction: A Meta-Analysis."

Ethical porn

Porn that is promoted as being more principled than other porn. Producers do not traffic or coerce performers, working conditions for actors are better than in the larger industry, and the films portray both real-world people and performers. Promoters claim that production and distribution stay within legal boundaries.

Regardless of the attempts to promote porn production as an ethical activity, it remains that porn is concerning, and all porn is addicting. A viewer can become just as hooked on watching real people have sex as he can viewing O-Mi's involving actors. Porn, in general, portrays people who are more attractive than the average population. This often leaves viewers feeling bad about their own and their partners' bodies. Porn watchers can also become increasingly dissatisfied with their sex lives because what they see on screen seems better than what they have with their partners (Paul, 2005). The portrayal of real-world couples sounds positive, but if the pattern follows the one seen on large porn sites, real-life partners might enact even more gender stereotypes (submissive and masochistic women and aggressive and dominant men) than is seen in "professionally" produced porn (see **gender inequality**) (Lehmiller, 2017).

Evolutionary theory

The theory that all organisms, including humans, evolve over time, and the better adapted they are, the more offspring they have (Than & Taylor, 2021).

Applied to porn, the obvious argument is that men want to look at pictures of young women of reproductive age. Sex and reproduction are fundamental aspects of human existence. On the other hand, pornography doesn't pass muster when considered from an evolutionary standpoint. An indication that evolutionary theory just doesn't work when applied to O-Mi viewing is that sex with real women becomes less frequent for the porn user (see **intercourse** and **sex recession** below). Porn viewers might be less likely to marry and reproduce; porn threatens **reproductive success**. Or consider **pubic hair**, which distinguishes mature from immature females. Since much porn wants to dispense with women's pubic hair and sometimes men's as well, it appears to ignore the evolutionary imperative that immature humans who (obviously) can't reproduce should not be sexually approached. To the extent that evolutionary theory can be applied to porn use at all, and particularly to porn **addiction**, it predicts lower evolutionary success.

Eyebounce

Looking away from sexual imagery.

Eyebounce is the opposite of ogle. **Ogling** involves seeing another person as an **object** for one's own enjoyment. Only by practicing eyebounce is it possible to be 100 percent **porn-free** and faithful to one's **romantic** partner. People who practice eyebounce do not look at O-Mi's. One porn addict said, "It felt strange doing this at first, but now looking away has become a new habit" (Maltz & Maltz, 2008, p. 175).

Fapping

Masturbating to pornography.

Fapping sites contain O-Mi's to masturbate to. A fapper is someone who looks at a lot of porn (see **ogling**) and masturbates to the O-Mi's he is viewing. How much a fapper masturbates probably varies by age, but assuming sexual function has not been compromised by his porn habit (see **erectile dysfunction** and **PIED**), it would be well beyond the average for other men of the same age (see **addiction** and **musterbator**).

Fear of aging

Anxiety about getting older.

Many men are concerned about getting older and think that viewing porn will keep them young. But if they have **erectile dysfunction** as a consequence (see **PIED**), the opposite will be the case. Not marrying or ending up **divorced** if they do (a frequent result of porn use) may also make them "older." They will age faster and perhaps die at a younger age than they otherwise would. I am basing this comment on the argument made by Dr. Michael F. Roizen, the close colleague of the famous Dr. Oz, that our life activities can make us age faster or slower. Consequently, our "real age" can be very different from our chronological age (Roizen, 2004).

Thus, men who fear aging should fear porn because it is likely that it will accelerate aging. Orgasms (with a partner or not) do help maintain sexual ability. However, the facts that O-Mi's negatively affect mental and emotional health and engender negative attitudes toward women suggest that porn use is not a path to sexual health (see **addiction**, **brain damage**, **Dr. Jekyll and Mr. Hyde**, **mental health**, **neuroscience**, **objects**, **ogling**, **oxytocin**, and **shorter lives**).

Female breast mutilation

Surgery performed to alter the size and shape of **healthy** breasts. The emphasis here is on *healthy*. Female breast mutilation is different than **breast reconstruction** used to recreate normal-looking breasts for women who have had their breasts removed or surgically altered due to cancer or other disease or injury.

Westerners frequently question the **female genital mutilation** that occurs in other cultures. However, considering the side-effects of unnecessary breast operations makes clear uncomfortable truths that many people have not been willing to think about (Zakaria, 2010). Eighty-five percent of women in the porn industry have had this type of surgery (Maltz & Maltz, 2008, p. 35) (see **cyborgs** and **cyborg femmes**). They are often not well informed beforehand about the possible side effects (Grudzen et al., 2009).

The surgery reduces sensation in the breast and nipple area (Newman, 2017) and involves a risk of scarring and capsular contracture. When contracture occurs, hard, dense tissue encapsulates the implant and squeezes it, causing chronic pain and changes in the breasts' appearance (*Capsular Contracture*, 2020). Implants can also rupture, interfere with nursing, and make it harder to detect breast cancer during mammography (Zakaria, 2010). They can feel uncomfortable and can leak. The breasts of a woman with implants may feel cool compared to the rest of her body and can be especially problematic in cold weather (Breastcancer.org Community, 2014).

Research on almost 100,000 women who have had this surgery suggests that silicone implants are associated with slightly higher rates of three conditions classified as autoimmune diseases: Sjögren's syndrome, scleroderma, and rheumatoid arthritis. In addition, the surgery is associated with stillbirths and melanoma (Wolters Kluwer Health, 2018).

Women who have had cancer or other breast disease or injury will usually get **breast reconstruction**, but some make other choices such as getting beautiful tattoos where their breasts were (Guthrie, n.d.). Our culture, however, tends to equate femaleness with breasts. Many women get breast reconstruction to feel better about themselves. It is also likely, however, that men's porn use makes the decision not to get implants more difficult since women often compare their bodies to those of entertainers and online sex models and performers, most of whom have implants (see **beautiful women** and **cyborg femmes**).

Female genital mutilation

The cutting, removal, or sewing closed of a female's external genitals. The purpose is to limit or eliminate women's sexual response or, in the case of online sex models and porn actors, to please males who want to view vulvas that are more diminutive and symmetrical than may be the case for many adult women.

Online models and porn performers may undergo a version of this surgery to enhance their job options and income. They may have the labia minora, the small inner folds of the vulva, surgically altered (labiaplasty) so that they are smaller and more evenly shaped. Side effects can include infection, scarring, and lessened genital sensation. The intent is to make the vulva "neat and tidy." No long-term evidence exists on the safety of these procedures (Creighton, 2014; Kirkman, 2019).

In summary, **female breast mutilation** and female genital mutilation, when done on healthy tissue, have significant side effects. The online sex world has created a demand for unusually shapely women (typically thin with breasts that are larger than expected given their general lack of body fat, though other body types are certainly also represented) and women whose genitals are unnaturally childlike. The awareness of women in the general population of the O-Mi images that men are viewing leads some of them to follow suit and seek these surgeries in order to look like surgically altered sex models and performers. They may then feel more confident in their appearance but may also have diminished sexual response (Grudzen et al., 2009) (see **sexy vs. sexual**).

Fetishes

A desire for uncommon sexual practices and images. The term is sometimes used only to refer to sex involving inanimate objects, but it also sometimes refers to **BDSM** and other paraphilias such as anal sex (see **intercourse** and **violence against women**).

Desire for this type of material is widespread in the porn world: "Even in mainstream porn, there is an incredible display of violence against women. In a content analysis of the 50 top-selling porn movies, 88 percent showed physical aggression toward women, primarily spanking, gagging, and slapping" (Grillo, 2021) (see **gender inequality**, **hard core**, **sexual deviance**, and **XXX**).

A lot of online porn encourages the development of fetishes. Some may be harmless though considered to be "**weird sex**" by most in the general population, including many porn users. Other fetishes can cause significant psychological and sometimes physical harm to those who participate. These desires will result in more difficulty in finding an actual partner because many potential partners will not want to participate in the fetish. The more unusual the fetish, the harder it will be to find willing partners. Some prospective partners may react with derision or even horror.

Though many porn users fear that the fetishes that have become a part of their O-Mi viewing indicate inherent predilections, those who quit porn often find that their desire for this material (and fetish activities) disappears within months (Wilson, 2017, p. 90). According to Dr. Mary Anne Layden (n.d.), a psychiatrist, they are psychiatric symptoms, but they are often reversible (see **mental health**).

Freedom

"Being able to make choices regarding your behavior that enable you to live your healthiest, happiest life" (Maltz & Maltz, 2008, p. 265).

While there are many definitions of freedom, I use this one because it focuses on health and happiness, which, as I noted in the introduction, are the underlying **values** of this book. It is also especially applicable to **addiction**. Wendy and Larry Maltz (2008), counselors, educators, and the authors of *The Porn Trap*, suggest that when discussing porn, the common definition of freedom as "being able to do whatever, whenever," and to act without restraint, is adolescent. Porn can limit the user's freedom. Maltz and Maltz (2008, pp. 255-266) go so far as to say that the porn addict is enslaved. The porn addict cannot live their happiest and healthiest life.

The women depicted in porn are not free either. They frequently perform while tied, chained, or handcuffed. Gagging is common; they certainly don't have **freedom of speech** (see **BDSM**). They mostly work in the industry for money but frequently endure significant physical and emotional abuse (Grudzen et al., 2009). Porn work is not making them free, healthy, or happy. Most would not work in the industry if they felt they had better options (see **solutions** in the conclusion).

Users who quit will increase their freedom in multiple ways. They will feel less **guilty** (having ended the damage to themselves and others). Since porn use can contribute to emotional dysfunction (see **mental health**), they will probably feel less depressed and anxious. They will have more freedom to do other things since porn is a huge time suck. And they have made the decision to quit; they are free from having to decide what they should do about their O-Mi habit. Though they may **relapse**, they have a new **identity** as a **porn-free guy**, and that can help them get back on track more readily. They are free to grow and evolve as a person in ways that porn may have limited.

If ending O-Mi viewing is tied to a transcendent value, such as fidelity to one's **romantic** partner, the decision to be porn-free may be more meaningful, more sustainable, and perhaps even more enjoyable (Peele, 2004; Peele, 2015; Rubin, 2015, pp. 141–142). Cravings for porn will decrease as viewing decreases.

Hence, freedom from porn will gradually increase as O-Mi use declines (see **compulsion**).

Freedom of speech

The right to publicly express opinions without being punished by the government.

In the United States, porn is protected by its designation as free speech. Hence, it is protected by the first amendment. Child pornography and **obscenity**, however, are not protected speech. Obscenity refers to sexual material that violates community standards and has no serious literary, artistic, political, or scientific value. A large proportion of porn fits the definition of obscenity, and child pornography is common and pursued by all age groups, including **iGen** (Maren, 2020), but currently, little enforcement occurs.

One possible **solution** to the porn epidemic is to update and publicize obscenity laws. Apprehension and prosecution of individuals in these cases is likely to be rare, just as it is for **drug** use, but having laws on the books that stigmatize obscenity as illegal is likely to lessen social acceptance. Thus, laws could help change the general view of porn and make the **environment**, likely the biggest factor in making porn less acceptable, less friendly to developing or continuing a viewing habit (Bradley, 2010, p. 215).

Fun

Something that provides amusement, enjoyment, or euphoria.

I was shocked when a user told me that porn often isn't fun. While the most common reasons given for seeking out porn involve **pleasure**, relieving psychological distress is not far behind (and may be preeminent) as a reason for using porn.

It seems likely that many users view O-Mi's both for sexual release and for emotional soothing. O-Mi's help users deal with loneliness, boredom, fears of inadequacy and rejection, depression, and anxiety (see **compulsion**, **defenses, psychological**, **Dr. Jekyll and Mr. Hyde**, **drugs**, and **mental health**).

An **addiction** causes a momentary euphoria that addresses an inner emptiness. Kasl suggests that addictions are a misguided search for self-love and spiritual fulfillment (see **religion**). What the addict really needs are caring **relationships,** social support (Kasl, 1989, p. 19), and meaningful activities, but porn is cheap (and often free), accessible, and anonymous (see **AAA**).

Gender inequality

The relative status and power of women and men. In all known societies, men have had higher status and power than women of their same class and race.

There is little research on gender inequality and male and female stereotypes in porn. A common view is that heterosexual porn is full of **old-fashioned** gender stereotypes: virgins, whores, and hypersexed men. To the extent that this is true, it is ironic that many users think that O-Mi viewing makes them "cool" and "up-to-date."

One of the few studies looking at gender inequality and porn found that women were more likely to be portrayed as submissive and masochistic and men as dominant and sadistic, though in about half the videos, there was no difference in power. There were more close-ups of female body parts (hence women were more likely to be portrayed as **objects** than were men), and more scenes focused on male **pleasure** than on female pleasure. Women were more likely to be spanked and gagged than men, though in the study referenced here, violence was relatively infrequent (Lehmiller, 2017) (see **BDSM**, **racial inequality**, **violence against women**, and **XXX**). Amateur pornography depicted more gender inequality than professional porn.

This study looked at four large porn sites. Since there are many more porn sites than four, its results are not necessarily representative of all internet porn.

Guilt

What we experience when we don't live up to our **values**. It is also felt when we don't live up to our obligations to other people, including **romantic** partners, children, and employers.

Guilt is a good thing if it causes the guilty person to make up for past wrongs and improve future behavior ("Guilt," n.d.). Some porn users may feel uncomfortable about their O-Mi viewing, which many people (including even some porn users) consider to be in conflict with values of faithfulness, respect for women, spirituality, and **love**. O-Mi addicts in **recovery** become aware of the damage they have done to their romantic partners, their children, and the women and men who work in the online sex industry.

Some porn users and addicts feel guilty for using porn. Ironically, their romantic partners may feel guilty if they try to *stop* their husband or boyfriend from O-Mi viewing. The porn user may try to make his girlfriend or wife feel guilty by saying that he has "male needs," and he is entitled to his privacy. But negative reactions from a romantic partner may save the **relationship** (see **divorce** and **environment**) and have positive **mental health** benefits for both partners.

In some cases, girlfriends or wives become their mate's **accountability partners**. For other porn viewers, their **therapist** or fellow **twelve-step program** members are a better choice. At any rate, the female partner of the male porn user has the right to the mental faithfulness (see **cheating**, **chipping**, and **mental infidelity**) of her partner and is justified if she tries to stop her partner's porn use. Part of his **recovery** will be to acknowledge his guilt in O-Mi viewing and its negative effects on him, his partner and their relationship, his children, and workers in the porn industry. He cannot emerge from his habit or **addiction** if he is in **denial**.

H.A.L.T.

An acronym used to help addicts avoid **relapse**. It reminds them to never become too **h**ungry, too **a**ngry, too **l**onely, or too **t**ired (Carnes, 1991, p. 285).

These circumstances can cause O-Mi addicts to crave porn, but of course, there are many other **triggers** that make it hard for the porn addict to abstain from porn.

Hard-core

Porn that depicts aggression or violence combined with sex. The aggression or violence is predominantly, but not only, by men against women.

A significant amount of what was once considered hard-core porn is now considered to be **soft-core** porn. In the past, hard-core porn would have been pictures of sexual intercourse (now considered soft-core), but the porn world has moved far beyond that. Much of hard-core porn portrays **BDSM** and anal sex, both of which are current fixations of many viewers, as well as many other paraphilias, including the sexual abuse of children.

According to Norman Doidge (2007, p. 102), hard-core pornography fuses sex with "hatred and humiliation." The hostility against women expressed by the male actors on these sites (and by the producers of this material) cannot be considered healthy, nor can the women's passive or seemingly welcoming acceptance of aggression and abuse. The female actors, however, may be drunk or high or may have been coerced by producers and male performers to act in a submissive and demeaning way (Grudzen et al., 2009) (see **fetishes**, **gender inequality**, **kink**, **mental health**, **Pornhub.com**, **racial inequality**, **violence against women**, and **XXX**).

Identity

How we view ourselves and our sense of being a particular way or of belonging to a particular group.

Identity can have a significant impact on whether we can **recover** from an **addiction**. A porn addict might take pride in thinking of himself as a bad boy, a rebel, or a sexual **freedom** fighter. These identities could make it hard to quit porn, even if they are negatively impacting his life. On the other hand, if he thinks of himself first and foremost as an altruist, a lover, a faithful husband, a father, or as a **porn-free guy** who wouldn't waste time on porn because he has better things to do, he may be better able to stop his O-Mi viewing.

Experts differ on whether a porn addict should continue to think of himself as a porn addict once he has stopped viewing O-Mi's. Most of them follow the **twelve-step** philosophy that continuing to think of oneself as a porn addict is essential to staying clear of an O-Mi habit and avoiding **relapse** (Smith, 2019). In contrast, Dr. Stanton Peele (2004, p. 172), while he sees twelve step groups as one viable route away from addiction, thinks that "assuming a new identity as a moral, responsible person" is a step toward making huge and life-affirming changes. Though changing one's self-image is not usually easy for an addict, Peele (2004, pp. 181–192) suggests that a view of oneself as a mature nonaddict who is leading a life consistent with his basic **values** is not only possible but desirable.

iGen

People born 1995 or later. They are also sometimes called Generation Z.

This group of people has grown up with smartphones (often iPhones, hence the label iGen) and with readily accessible porn on their phones and other electronic devices. Many members of iGen were exposed to porn at an early age, as well as to the attitudes associated with the online sex world.

Many of the **values** pushed by online sex sites are far removed from the values that have supported **love**, **romance**, **relationships**, and marriage. An acceptance of casual sex and a preference for love-free relationships, often arising from a desire for independence or a focus on self-development, have accompanied the heavy O-Mi viewing habits of many in the iGen age group. Not surprisingly, this highly individualistic perspective and the lack of love and support that result have led to high rates of depression, anxiety, and suicide among iGen's (see **mental health**). Also, iGen's are less **religious** than past generations, so many of them lack that bulwark against porn use (Twenge, 2017, Ch. 5). It also appears that iGen's have less sex with real people than earlier generations (see **sex recession**), possibly because of their porn use (Pappas, 2012; Twenge, 2017, Chs. 4, 8; Wilcox & Stone, 2019).

Infidelity Survivors Anonymous (ISA)

This **twelve-step** group is for **romantic** partners who have "experienced infidelity induced trauma caused by any form of sexual betrayal in their relationships." This includes porn use (see

cheating, **chipping**, **fapping**, and **musterbator**), as well as affairs and casual sex with actual women by a sex-addicted partner.

Intercourse

Sex with actual body contact between individuals and penetration.

The vaginal-penile version of this behavior, necessary for **reproduction**, appears to decrease as porn use and **addiction** increase. As porn use increases, the brain becomes rewired, and the reward system that is normally linked to sex is now linked to porn. To put it bluntly, porn is killing sex (Wilson, 2017, p. 6) (see **brain damage**, **erectile dysfunction**, **evolutionary theory**, **neuroscience**, **PIED**, **reproductive success**, and **voyeur**).

Heterosexual anal-penile intercourse is a very common **fetish** on the internet. Women working in the porn industry often strive to avoid it, though they can earn more money if they engage in it (Grudzen et al., 2009). Its ubiquity online has led to more experimentation with this practice among the general population, but not necessarily to increased sexual enjoyment. A 2014 British qualitative study on anal sex among young participants (ages 16-18) found "few young men or women reported finding anal sex pleasurable and both expected anal sex to be painful for women." The two main reasons given for having this kind of sex was that the young men wanted to copy what they had seen on porn sites and expected that the anus would be "tighter" than a **vagina** (Regnerus & Uecker, 2011, p. 94; Wilson, 2017, p. 181).

Intimacy

"The skill of being physically, emotionally, spiritually, and mentally connected with someone else and the world around us and maintaining that connection" (Pearsall, 1994, p. 36).

Porn use typically involves lying and hiding (see **denial**, **Dr. Jekyll and Mr. Hyde**, **dupes**, and **trust**) and lessens intimacy in the user's **romantic** **relationship**, if he has one. Or it may substitute for having a **love** relationship altogether.

The word *skill* in the definition is important; intimacy is not something that we are born knowing how to do. Our earliest relationships with caregivers prime us for healthy or less healthy relationships and sexuality later in our lives (Doidge, 2007, Ch. 4). Adult relationships, however, involve some skills learned only when we are teens and adults. If porn users are not having romantic relationships (see **iGen** and **sex recession**), then they will not become skillful at sexual intimacy. Substituting porn for relationships will often lead to more loneliness and depression and may well deepen the user's porn **addiction**.

Note that this definition suggests that healthy intimacy requires not only a close connection with another (not necessarily with a romantic partner) but a strong, multifaceted sense of connection with our **environment**—"the world around us." To be healthy people capable of intimacy, we must exist in a positive web of connection and community. If we exist in a porn-infused environment that discourages love and intimacy, our connections will be weak, and our **mental health** will be poor. The friends of a porn addict may deride romantic connections and suggest that love relations are likely to be short-lived or impossible. Or they may question relationships with women who don't look like the O-Mi's that they view online. Being tethered to the porn pictures on electronic devices will not allow the viewer to develop the resources necessary to be healthy or happy.

Intimacy dysfunction

The inability to connect with someone else physically, emotionally, spiritually, and mentally over time. It also (again using Paul Pearsall's definition of **intimacy**) includes an inability to have a multifaceted connection with the world around us and the lack of a positive web of connection with a community.

According to sex **addiction** expert Dr. Patrick Carnes, porn addicts are typically afflicted with intimacy dysfunction (Smith, 2019, pp. 3-4). Intimacy dysfunction is caused by childhood abuse or neglect—or by porn itself. People with this dysfunction avoid the vulnerability of real-life intimacy. If they have a relationship, they "fuck" rather than make love. They seek constant sexual highs. When having sex or when using porn to get a neurochemical rush, they feel alone and often sad. They then seek further sexual highs and feel even worse. They are addicted to sex partly because they lack the skills to connect in a caring **relationship**. They connect largely or even only on a physical level (Kasl, 1989, pp. 268-269; Pearsall, 1994, pp. 177-178).

This suggests that people who experienced neglect or abuse in childhood may be especially vulnerable to porn addiction. However, viewing internet porn often leads to addiction even in people with healthier childhoods. Research in **neuroscience** suggests that internet porn is uniquely suited to change the brain (see **brain damage**) and the body's neurocircuitry in ways that earlier porn could not do. The result is addiction (Smith, 2019).

Johns

Men who purchase sexual services. They are also called **tricks** (and in Great Britain, punters).

Virtual johns are men who use porn; they may subscribe to the personal porn sites of **virtual prostitutes** or subscribe to or get free porn, which is paid for by the advertisers on large porn sites (see **Pornhub.com** for an example). Without johns and their pursuit of porn, the O-Mi industry would not exist (see **Big porn**).

The demand for sexual services, including porn, exists for many reasons. Some porn users do not have a **romantic** partner and do not want one. Others want a partner but haven't been able to attract or keep one. Some have **fetishes** that most women don't want to accommodate. Some are thrill-seekers. Some are curious about what's out there. Some want the experience of having sex with women that they would never be able to attract in real life. Often, they don't realize that **virtual pimps** and male porn actors treat women in the sex business in hurtful ways, or that some of the girls and women are underage and **trafficked** (Smith & Vardaman, 2010) (see **lawsuits**, **legal, prostitution,** and **violence against women**). Porn users who do have romantic partners generally realize that their partner may be uneasy with, and often very much opposed to, their online sex activity (Paul, 2005; Pappas, 2012).

A key way to cut the demand for porn would be to make it less **affordable** (see **AAA**). Taxing O-Mi viewing is one option. As far as I can discern, only one bill of this type has been put forward in the U.S. Congress, and it would not impact current porn users (Folley, 2019). Activists and the government, however, could likely come up with some additional proposals to ensure that online sexual viewing is not free. Internet service that supplies access to these images, for example, could be made substantially more costly than internet service that doesn't (see **solutions** in the conclusion).

Kink

<u>Sexually deviant</u> practices and paraphilias, which include **<u>BDSM</u>** (bondage, domination/discipline, sadism/submission, and masochism), anal sex, and sex with children, as well as other less usual sexual practices.

Some of these practices may have origins in childhood sexual trauma, at least for some people who get fixated on them, but it is also clear that porn encourages desires that people never imagined that they could have (Doidge, 2007, 2013). Images of kink are almost always images of men degrading women and not the other way around (Gobry, 2019).

Much of the public (even those who watch kink online) consider it to be **"weird sex"** and **<u>fetishism</u>**. Porn frequently involves images of kink. Watching it can make it more acceptable to the watcher, who is then more likely to try to involve partners in these practices.

Many people, however, may remain **<u>voyeurs</u>** and feel unwilling to do personally what Twenge (2017, p. 213) has characterized as **"cruel sex."** For these people, watching kink may be something like watching a violent or bizarre nonsexual movie; watching doesn't mean that they want to enact what they are seeing. And as noted earlier, some O-Mi viewers no longer desire sex with other humans at all. Succinctly put, "porn kills sex" (Wilson, 2017, p. 6). The body becomes rewired for porn rather than for sexual connection (Volkow et al., 2016) (see **<u>gender inequality</u>**, **<u>hard-core</u>**, **<u>intercourse</u>**, **<u>racial inequality</u>**, **<u>sex recession</u>**, and **<u>XXX</u>**).

Lawsuits

A case in a court of law in which one party makes a complaint against another.

Victims of online sexual abuse can take the porn company

executives and online male sex actors who abuse them to court to be compensated for the damage done to them.

In 2019, twenty-two women won nearly $13 million in a lawsuit against GirlsDoPorn, claiming that executives of the porn site acted deceptively to get them into shoots, intimidated them into performing, and shared their images online without their agreement. The executives were found liable for fraud and breach of contract (Hassan & Syckle, 2019). Further development in the case occurred in June 2021, when GirlsDoPorn producer Andre Garcia was sentenced to 20 years in prison for sex **trafficking** (STATEMENT: GirlsDoPorn Producer Rightly Sentenced, 2021).

Litigation will become a major route for changing the porn scene, just as it has been in challenging tobacco companies. The National Center on Sexual Exploitation has filed multiple cases against large porn companies like MindGeek and the WebGroup Czech Republic and their respective subsidiaries, including **Pornhub.com** and XVideos.com (*Our Cases*, n.d.). Trafficking, coercion, and child porn are central issues in these lawsuits, which can be expected to improve the behavior of the porn industry and limit the material available to users.

Legal

The age of majority at which one is considered to be an adult. In most countries this is 18. Before this age, a minor cannot consent to appear in porn shoots.

Some online sex models and performers are nonadults (under 18), and some of them have been **trafficked**. Thus, the images of these girls and women have been obtained illegally. It is often impossible to know who is an illegal porn victim. Beware of teen sites; they are the most popular sites for porn users, and it is often the case that some of the young women on those sites have been trafficked. One indication of the merit of these concerns is **Pornhub.com**'s removal of over 75 percent of its films in 2020. The company executives appeared to fear **lawsuits** and ongoing negative publicity such as that which appeared in the *New York Times* (Kristof, 2020).

The search for barely mature females is a concerning part of "legitimate" porn use. Users who would never knowingly get involved in child porn may visit mostly teen sites (Trafficking Hub, n.d.). As men fall deeper into a porn habit or **addiction,** some become more and more obsessed with looking for "barely legal" young women—or for images that are illegal but labeled legal. They may want to maintain a self-image of normalcy but at the same time are risking going over the boundaries into child porn (see **identity**).

Some experts suggest that teenagers are not prepared to deal with the multiple risks and challenges found in the porn industry and that performers should be required to be at least 21 years of age (Grudzen et al., 2009, p. 78).

Love

The act of caring for other people, including our sexual partners. It is also a transcendent *value* that, if emphasized in a person's life, may help cure a porn **addiction**.[4]

Caring **relationships** and love are needed for a happy, fulfilled life. Porn can keep the user from finding and retaining **romantic** love. Some men cannot "settle" for women close to their own age or for women who don't approach the appearance

---

4 See Ravi Chandra's article "A Possible Cure for Pornography Addiction—In an Essay," in *Psychology Today*, Jan. 24, 2012, https://www.psychologytoday.com/us/blog/the-pacific-heart/201201/possible-cure-pornography-addiction-in-essay. This is a summary of David Mura's classic essay, "A Male Grief: Notes on Pornography and Addiction." Similar views are expressed by Stanton Peele in "12 Concepts of Recovery that Have Stood the Test of Time," April 11, 2015, https://www.thefix.com/content/12-ways-overcome-your-or-others addictions.

of online sex models and performers. When porn users do get into a relationship, their O-Mi viewing may result in breakups or **divorce**.

Porn is almost always detrimental to love relationships (Gottman & Gottman, 2016). Romantic partners often feel they are in competition with online sex models and performers. The porn user's sexual energies are dispersed around the internet rather than focused on their partner. The partner is likely to feel neglected, and in the most serious cases of addiction, may have a boyfriend or husband who is largely absent from the relationship because of his porn use. In this situation, **Mr. Hyde** constitutes the larger part of a man's persona; **Dr. Jekyll** is in retreat. It is Dr. Jekyll who loves his partner, not Mr. Hyde. In addition, the porn user may lose his ability to get erections with a real-life partner, and eventually with O-Mi's as well (see **erectile dysfunction**, **pornified**, and **PIED**). As noted earlier, porn kills sex (Wilson, 2017, p. 6). It also kills love.

Maturing out

Outgrowing an **addiction** or a bad habit.

Addictive behavior is self-centered as an addict can only focus on himself and what he needs. According to addiction expert Stanton Peele (2004),

> addiction is a search for immature gratifications—it is self-seeking behavior resembling that of a dependent child. [O]vercoming addiction requires growing up and assuming adult roles (and taking) responsibility not only for yourself and your own behavior but for other people in your life.

Some psychologists suggest that pornography is an **immature defense mechanism** (Stansvik, 2018; Vaillent, 2012).

Research in neuroscience suggests that pornography viewing causes the brain to revert to an immature state (*Watching Pornography Rewires the Brain*, 2019).

Mature males have a better chance of finding and continuing **relationships**. Most **romantic** partners appreciate a mate who is sexually and emotionally focused on them and who does not split emotional connection from sexuality (see **repression**). In short, a mature male is capable of deep **intimacy** with a partner. Indulging in a porn habit will ensure that the brain remains in a juvenile state, with **intimacy dysfunction** being one sign of immaturity.

Mental health

Mental well-being.

Online porn performers, O-Mi users and addicts, and the wives and girlfriends of O-Mi users and addicts may be less mentally healthy than many people in the general population.

Information on the mental health of online sex models and performers is limited, and samples are typically biased in one direction or another. Longitudinal studies to assess the mental health of online porn performers over time would be insightful: What is the mental health of porn actors entering the industry? How are they faring by mid-career? How healthy are they when their careers end (which for most will be within three years)? Their mental health may vary significantly by the amount of time that they work in the business, as well as by whether they work in **soft-core** or **hard-core** pornography (Mooney, 2019).

Many of the women working in porn try to avoid the most brutal jobs and the most violent male actors (Grudzen, 2019), and this attests positively to their mental health. It also suggests that both the male actors and the men who seek this material online have significant mental health issues (see **fetishes**, **kink**, **sexual deviance**, and **violence against women**).

It appears, however, that the background of some of the female models and actors makes them more vulnerable to poor mental health than other women. As children, more of them experience rape, live in poverty, or are in foster care. Female porn actors have significantly higher rates of depression than other women of similar ages (Grillo, 2021; Grudzen et al., 2011). The abuse that some of them experienced as children may also make them more vulnerable to abuse when they work in the porn industry.

Actors are more likely to have personality disorders than the general population (Davison & Furnham, 2018), and it is possible that this finding applies to porn actors as well as to other actors. People with histrionic personality disorder, for example, tend toward exhibitionism, are sexually provocative, dramatic, and seek excitement and attention. They are also typically anxious and depressed (*Cluster B Personality Disorder*, n.d.). Posing or performing online and having many men **ogle** them appears to fit the sexually provocative and attention-seeking parts of their personalities. There is also some evidence that people with personality disorders are more oriented toward **BDSM** than people without personality disorders (Neef et al., 2019).

This inclination toward BDSM reflects a scrambling of the neurological paths of aggression and sexuality (Doidge, 2007, Ch. 4), paths that are meant to be separate. It is not a sign that people with personality disorders are sexually more "with it" than other people. Instead, it is one indication of their mental health diagnosis. Since they may already have a proclivity toward BDSM, performing it online might be more acceptable to them than to those without personality disorders.

On the other side of the porn equation, porn users and addicts frequently use O-Mi viewing to deal with depression, anxiety, boredom, and trauma (see **defenses, psychological**). There are obviously better ways to do this, but porn is cheap and easy. Porn, however, can worsen the depression and anxiety of the user. Thus, what is used as a **solution** may turn toxic and worsen their mental health (*Watching Pornography Rewires the Brain*, 2019).

The girlfriends and wives of porn users and addicts may also suffer psychologically. They may feel betrayal, mistrust, depression, and anger. They may require psychological treatment for **trauma**. Many of them compare themselves to online sex models and performers and feel unattractive and unable to compete sexually (Paul, 2005). Since porn users separate sex from **intimacy**, at least some of the time, women in a **relationship** with a porn user or addict may feel that their sexual life (if it continues, which it may not), with the porn user lacks warmth and closeness (Effects of Pornography on Marriage, n.d.) (see **cheating**, **divorce**, **Dr. Jekyll and Mr. Hyde**, **dupes**, **erectile dysfunction**, **Infidelity Survivors Anonymous (ISA)**, **intimacy**, **intimacy dysfunction**, **mental infidelity**, **PIED**, **pornified**, **repression**, and **trust**).

Mental infidelity

A state of mind where one imagines sexual encounters with O-Mi's or others who are not one's **romantic** partner. It is also referred to as **visual infidelity** (Layden, n.d.).

Pornography glamorizes cheating through films such as *Cheating Housewives*. But any porn, including porn "stills" of a lone female, will spark fantasies of having sex with people who are not one's mate; the O-Mi images do not need to focus on cheating to have that effect.

Thus, cheating begins in the mind. All infidelity, including mental infidelity, is problematic for **relationships** (see **cheating**, **chipping**, **divorce**, **fapping**, **hard-core**, **musterbator**, **soft-core**, and **trust**). Porn use is mental infidelity. On the other hand, **mental monogamy** supports relationships (see **eye bounce**).

The romantic partners of porn users are more likely to consider O-Mi viewing to be cheating than are porn users. Girlfriends and wives who don't consider O-Mi viewing to be mental infidelity are still often uneasy with their partner's porn habit (see **chick repellent**). This appears to be true in all age groups, even among young women who have grown up during the **porn pandemic** (Pappas, 2012; Regnerus & Uecker, 2011).

Moneyshot

A scene in a pornographic film where a man ejaculates. An angry—and common—version of the moneyshot is the **"pop face,"** where the male performer splatters the female's face (Faludi, 1999, 543) (see **gender inequality**, **hard-core**, **violence against women**, **woodsman**, and **XXX**).

Musterbater

Someone who masturbates **compulsively**.

They may be a **fapper**, though obsessive masturbation can occur without viewing O-Mi's. It does, however, often involve looking at O-Mi's (see **cheating**, **chipping**, and **ogling**).

Neuroscience

A life science that deals with the anatomy, biochemistry, and physiology of the nervous system.

Research in neuroscience is helping us understand how porn **addiction** works and what its effects are. Dr. Patrick Carnes, "the world's leading expert on sex addiction" (Smith, 2019, pp. 1-2), says that the neuroscience literature is "very, very clear" about the problems created by addiction, including porn addiction. Multiple online sites exist to familiarize the layperson with this research. Here are a few examples: Your Brain on Porn, Fight the New Drug, and RewardFoundation.org.

Recent research suggests that changes in neurocircuitry caused by porn viewing lead to **erectile dysfunction**, damaged executive function, and declines in **willpower** and impulse control. Though much of the damage can be reversed by abstaining from O-Mi viewing, this is proving more difficult in men whose viewing habits started in or before the teen years (Love et al., 2015; *Watching Pornography Rewires the Brain*, 2019; Wilson, 2019) (see **brain damage**, **mental health**, and **PIED**).

Nose jobs

Surgery that changes the shape of one's nose.

If online sex models and performers follow what was typical in the 21st century Playboy Mansion, many have had nose jobs to make their noses cute and pert (read "stereotypically female caucasian" looking). As noted earlier, the pornography and plastic surgery industries are closely intertwined (Madison, 2015; Maltz & Maltz, 2008; St. James, 2006) (see **beautiful women**, **cyborgs**, **cyborg femmes**, and **racial inequality**).

Object

A nonhuman form.

Research suggests that O-Mi viewers respond to the women in sexual imagery as objects. Most people viewing porn are not interested in the humanness of the people behind the images. Rather they seek impersonal sexual release and an escape from boredom and personal pain (Heflick & Goldenberg, 2014) (see **defenses, psychological**, **fapping**, **intimacy dysfunction**, **mental health**, **ogling**, and **repression**).

Obscenity

In June 1973, the U. S. Supreme Court issued a ruling that established a three-part test for defining obscenity as material that appeals to prurient interest, portrays sexual conduct "in a patently offensive way," and does not have "serious literary, artistic, political, or scientific value" (*The Supreme Court Defines Obscenity*, n.d.)

Disagreement about particular O-Mi's will, of course, exist, and a former Supreme Court justice (Potter Stewart) famously said about obscenity, "I know it when I see it." Nonetheless, a large proportion of porn fits the U.S. Supreme Court's definition.

The U.S. Department of Justice's persistent failure to prosecute federal obscenity laws has, until recently, given pornographers carte blanche to show whatever kinds of sexual imagery they want on the internet, with the exception of child porn. To retain their audience, pornographers have put porn that is increasingly violent, racist, and sexist on their sites. But **Pornhub.com**'s 2020 removal of over 75 percent of its films suggests that pornographers have less freedom over the materials they make available than they did in the past (see **freedom of speech**, **gender inequality**, **hard-core**, **pain**, **racial inequality**, **suffering**, **violence against women**, and **XXX**).

Ogling

Objectifying the bodies of others by staring with obvious sexual interest.

Ogling is part of porn use and **addiction**. The user or addict looks at sexual images and often masturbates to them. Consequently, I have used the term O-Mi: **o**gle **m**asturbatory **i**mage (see **fapping** and **musterbater**). **Porn guys** practice ogling; **porn-free guys** practice the opposite, which is **eye bounce**. When practicing eyebounce, a person looks away from sexual imagery instead of looking for it and at it (Maltz & Maltz, 2008, p. 175).

A 2014 study found that men who ogle use fewer human words such as "intelligent" or "kind" to describe women. The part of the brain that is activated when looking at inanimate **objects** is also activated by staring at females in a sexual way. Women with partners who ogle women feel less secure about their looks and their **relationships**. Thus, ogling harms the ogler's **romantic** partner, his bond with her, and his ability to see all women as full human beings. To say it is "just looking" is to avoid the significant issues and dehumanization that results from ogling (Heflick & Goldenberg, 2014) (see **gender inequality**).

An addict needs to practice careful "eyeball management." This is not easy for someone who has scored hundreds or even thousands of O-Mi hits a week. The **three-second rule** can help the porn user move toward eye bounce rather than ogling. The user looks away from the **triggering** image or person within three seconds, does not go back for another look, and then thinks about the other person as someone's daughter, wife, or sister, mentally sending that individual and his or her family his sincere best wishes (Brassart, 2020).

O-Mi (pronounced Oh My! with eyes popping)

<u>O</u>gle-<u>M</u>asturbatory <u>I</u>mage.

"Porn" has no agreed-upon definition, so O-Mi is a useful acronym, which includes two activities that are typically part of porn use, "**ogle**" and "masturbation." The term is broad enough to cover everything from the ***Sports Illustrated Swimsuit*** images that many people (probably more men than women) argue "are not porn" to the hardest core, most brutal films on **Pornhub. com**. Though these images are highly variable, they are all about escape, titillation, and for those who have **romantic** partners, **mental infidelity**.

The brain doesn't know what porn is (Wilson, 2017, p. 108), and the heated debates about porn's definition are beside the point. Instead, the crucial issue is the body's reaction to the images, whether they are of men handcuffing, slapping, and urinating on women, bra and panty ads, or multiple other "sexual" online images. There are men (though not necessarily the same men) who ogle, **edge**, and masturbate to all of them.

Oxytocin

A powerful human bonding hormone, created by the hypothalamus gland and released with orgasm "establishing a lasting emotional attachment with whomever, *or whatever*, you happen to be with or thinking about at the time" (Maltz & Maltz, 2008, p. 23). It is the neurochemical that leads to **intimate** connection.

According to Dr. Craig Hassed (2017, p. 97), humans, many primates, and prairie voles "have brains loaded with receptors for the hormone oxytocin...This receptor profile primes the species for long-standing, monogamous relationships" despite the counter operation of the **Coolidge effect** (which suggests that men are driven by a desire for sexual novelty). Paul Pearsall (1994, p. 150), a neuropsychologist who held that humans are programmed for monogamy, suggested that the human desire for sexual variety can be fulfilled through the many variations that one partner embodies on their "genetically programmed main theme." That is, one partner, explored thoroughly in an intimate **relationship**, will exhibit unique and varying traits and behaviors that can keep intimacy fresh and interesting.

Oxytocin can therefore be part of the answer to the craving for the neurochemical hits that characterize porn **addiction**. It can substitute for these hits, which come in spikes, as the porn user clicks from one O-Mi to the next. For those with a **loving** connection with a girlfriend or wife, oxytocin is released more slowly and results in a more sustainable high than the neuro-chemical rush associated with porn. It is thus possible to become "addicted" (or at least strongly bonded) to a lover and have a fulfilling relationship based on an oxytocin connection (Love, 2016). Preliminary research suggests that the large amount of oxytocin experienced in such a loving relationship may benefit the brain and memory (Tokyo University of Science, 2020) in contrast to the **brain damage** that occurs with porn addiction (see **fear of aging**, **mental health**, and **neuroscience**).

Pain

An unpleasant sensory experience ranging from mild discomfort to agony. The term can refer to physical sensation, emotional experience, or both.

Though one might think that the main goal of porn is **pleasure**, it is often used to address pain, loneliness, and even trauma (see **defenses, psychological** and **mental health**). For heavier users and addicts, their porn habit can result in a life of **trauma**. They may lose **relationships**, jobs, and even friends who don't approve of their activities if discovered. On the other side of the porn relationship, the acts required to keep up the physical appearance of an online female sex performer (such as breast augmentation, genital surgery, liposuction, **nose jobs**, and bikini waxes) are sources of pain to the performer. Many women are also abused, physically and emotionally, by the **virtual pimps** who run the industry and by the online male actors with whom they make films (Grudzen et al., 2008).

Porn users may ask their **romantic** partners to change their appearance via surgery or other painful procedures so that they look more like online O-Mi's (Paul, 2005). They may ask them to perform masochistic and often painful acts that they have seen online sex actors do (see **BDSM**, **fetishes**, **kink**, and **sexual deviance**). Thus, there are negative impacts on girlfriends and wives. The belief that women are essentially submissive and enjoy domination, humiliation, and pain is widespread in the porn world (see **gender inequality**, **racial inequality**, **suffering**, **violence against women**, and **XXX**). Mentally healthy women enjoy none of these things.

PIED

Porn-induced **erectile dysfunction**.

There is now a significant amount of evidence from **neuroscience** suggesting that even very young men are developing PIED and having difficulty having sex with real women, even though they may continue to masturbate and have orgasms when viewing O-Mi's (Gobry, 2019). In time, orgasm from porn use may also become difficult or impossible (Daubney, 2017) (see **pornified**).

A play on words might bring home this point. We might consider if porn is the 21st-century **PIED** Piper. In the 13th century, the Pied Piper is said to have played enchanting music that led to the disappearance of the rats infesting the village of Hamelin, Germany, and also lured 130 innocent children into a mountain when he did not get his expected pay. They were never seen again (Grey, 2019). Is the seductive song of porn leading many astray and into a deadly hidden place, away from the fulfilling lives that they should have? When we say it's time to "pay the piper," a saying which likely also derives from the legend, we might be referring to PIED, which results from the seductive song of porn.

Pimps

Someone, usually a man, who manages and often controls one or more **prostitutes** and who earns a living by taking some or all of the money paid by **johns** to those prostitutes for sex.

In the online sex world, **virtual pimps** earn their living by controlling porn sites and the women and men who pose for pictures or act in the sex films available on the sites (see **virtual prostitutes**). The sites may require **virtual johns** to subscribe to them for a fee, or money might come from advertisers so that the virtual johns can see the sexual images for free.

Pleasure

Enjoyment, euphoria, a positive emotional or physical sensation.

People enjoy porn; they feel euphoric from the various neurochemicals released during porn use. Pleasure, however, is not the only reason that men view O-Mi's. Porn use may also be a way of addressing boredom, emotional pain, trauma, and loneliness (see **defenses, psychological**, and **mental health**).

The pleasures of porn may prove elusive. O-Mi users and addicts may experience a lot of pleasure from porn but may, over time, have increasing difficulty enjoying life's other pleasures. Like **drugs**, porn can desensitize users by overwhelming the brain with **dopamine** and other neurochemicals. The user starts to lose appreciation of the nonsexual things that they used to find **fun** or exciting. (Wilson, 2017, p. 83)

The sexual images they enjoyed during the early stages of porn use may cease to spark the highs that they did initially. In time, some users may view more aggressive and violent images so that they can attain the pleasurable feelings they want from porn (Doidge, 2007, Ch. 4; Wilson, 2017) (see **gender inequality**, **hard-core**, **racial inequality**, **violence against women**, and **XXX**).

Porn users also compromise their happiness (a more global and broader emotion than pleasure) when porn use or **addiction** undercuts their **relationships**, their work, and the goals that they will never reach because of the time they spend on porn (See the cartoon included with the entry on **smoking** below.) Consequently, O-Mi viewing may supply pleasure but diminish happiness (Wilcox & Stone, 2019).

Porn

A word with a variety of definitions. Consequently, though used in this document because of its wide use and because readers are familiar with it, it is not defined here (and, therefore, also not underlined or put in bold in other entries).

"O-Mi" replaces or is used with it in parts of this book because it has a much clearer definition than "porn." O-Mi is an acronym that includes the two activities most associated with viewing sex images: **O**gling and **M**asturbation (see **chick repellent**, **fapping**, **hard-core**, **obscenity**, **soft-core**, and **XXX**).

Pornaholic

A porn addict. Someone who cannot control a **compulsion** to view O-Mi's (see **addiction** and **freedom**).

Just as alcoholics are addicted to alcohol, pornaholics are addicted to porn. Pornaholics get pixilated on pixels, just as alcoholics get drunk on booze, and heroin addicts get high on heroin. All of these addicts may be headed for **brain damage**, **erectile dysfunction**, damaged **relationships**, and **divorce**.

Porn blockers

Software that limits access to porn sites.

These blockers are used for children and adults. When used to block children, the intent is usually to prevent O-Mi viewing and **addiction**. When used to block adults, the intent is more likely to curb an addiction that already exists. Porn blockers also help make room for other tasks and life activities since viewing porn sites can take up a great deal of time. (See the cartoon included with the entry on **smoking** below.) Keeping unblocked electronic gadgets, including unblocked smart TVs (see **shock machines**) around when you are trying to kick a porn habit is equivalent to keeping junk food on your nightstand when you are trying to lose weight.

If you are an **accountability partner** who has administrative access to a porn blocker site but who needs technical help, expect to use the chat services and email advice that are available with all porn blockers. They can be an enormous help. There is a learning curve for all porn blocker software. Also, beware of Virtual Private Networks (**VPN**s). One of the major functions of a VPN is to bypass porn blockers.

Porn-free guy

A man who practices **eyebounce** and looks away from sexual images rather than seeking them out.

A porn-free guy does not objectify women or make them into **objects**. He does not see women's bodies as there to serve him and give him a neurochemical rush whenever he desires it, and he does not collect a harem of pictures and sex films on his computer or other electronic devices (see **shock machines**). He also blocks **XXX**, NC-17, and sexually focused NR films on his smart TV, and if he is overcoming an **addiction**, he is cautious about other **triggers**, including some R films and TV-MA programs (see **bottom feeder films and TV programs**).

According to Maltz and Maltz (2008, p. 190), authors of *The Porn Trap*, "the ultimate goal of porn recovery is to be in and stay in the Porn-Free Zone. This is where you have absolutely no involvement with porn, mentally or physically, and are not troubled by porn in any way."

Porn guy

A man who uses porn. He seeks out O-Mi's and may store sexual images on his electronic devices (see **shock machines**).

Most women would rather be with a **porn-free guy** than with someone who uses—even a little. And most women will avoid heavy users. Once more people know the research on the effect of porn on **relationships**, many will likely be wary of getting involved with porn users and addicts. As Gobry (2019) suggests, "[G]iven what porn **addiction** does to male sexuality, from the female perspective, sex with a male porn addict sounds like an experiment you don't want to repeat" (see **cheating**, **chick repellent**, **chipping**, **divorce**, **love**, and **romance**).

Since "nice guys" use porn, and porn users hide, there's no telling who the porn user is. They might be that sweet person sitting next to you in church, the church's minister, an innocent appearing teenager, or someone who is in late middle or old age. Or maybe you are **Dr. Jekyll and Mr. Hyde** and hiding your secret porn life. Outing your inner porn guy—Mr. Hyde—will lead to greater mental and, perhaps, physical health (Weaver et al., 2011) (see **erectile dysfunction**, **mental health**, **neuroscience**, **PIED**, **recovery**, and **shorter lives**).

It is usually a stop and start process, helped by a reaffirmation of the porn user's deepest **values** and by **therapists**, **accountability partners**, **porn blockers**, **twelve-step** programs, and an **environment** that does not support O-Mi viewing (see **solutions** in the conclusion).

Pornhub.com

The largest pornography website on the Internet.

Much of what is available on the site can be classified as **hard-core** porn and **XXX** videos. There is a significant amount of **violence against women**. The site has no system to verify that those pictured have consented to the acts depicted or have even reached adulthood. Consequently, it is likely that some of the Pornhub.com models and actors have been **trafficked** and are not there of their own volition and that some of them are minors (see **legal**).

In December 2020, Pornhub.com removed over 10 million unverified videos, over 75 percent of its collection. This was likely due to increased negative attention in the media and government actions against the company (Kristof, 2020; Mickelwait, 2021).

In February 2021, NCOSE filed a lawsuit in Montreal, Quebec, against MindGeek subsidiaries, including Pornhub.com, seeking damages for all people whose films or photos had been posted to websites overseen by MindGeek entities without their permission (Hawkins, 2021).

In June 2021, a RICO lawsuit was filed against Pornhub.com. and its parent company MindGeek.[5] The suit accuses the companies of monetizing child pornography and of operating as a "classic criminal enterprise" (Brown Rudnick, 2021).

Pornhub.com is also referred to as **Traffickinghub** by people attempting to hold its executives accountable for the trafficking of victims and for violence against women and children appearing on Pornhub.com (Trafficking Hub, n.d.) (see **Big porn** and **virtual pimps**).

---

5 Racketeer Influenced and Corrupt Organizations Act, 18 U.S.C. §§ 1961-68 (1970).

Note: there are many other pornography internet sites, but I mention Pornhub.com because it is one of the best known and most used.

Pornified

An obsession with sexual imagery, occuring both in cultures as a whole and individuals. In pornified cultures, sexual images are hard to avoid, and viewing O-Mi's is thought to be chic and cool (Paul, 2005). Porn is so common that it has been described as a tsunami by Dr. Mary Anne Layden (Shea, 2015).

It also describes what happens to porn users. They experience a change in their preferences when it comes to the physical appearance of sexual and marital partners, sexual activities, and in some cases, in their sexual abilities.

For example, some pornified males insist that females shave their **pubic hair**, a "taste" they have developed through their O-Mi viewing. Others develop **erectile dysfunction** (**PIED**) and lose their ability to perform sexually with normal females. Hugh Hefner, though surrounded by "playmates" and "bunnies" (all of whom were **cyborg femmes** as described above), could only have orgasms if he concluded his sexual activity by looking at porn (Madison, 2015; St. James, 2006).

Porn pandemic

The worldwide epidemic of O-Mi viewing. The "**sexual tsunami**" (Shea, 2015) of internet porn.

An interest in erotic images has always existed in human societies, but the pandemic is caused by the **Triple A Engine of Porn**: computers have made O-Mi images widely accessible and affordable, and have rendered O-Mi viewers anonymous (see **AAA: accessibility, anonymity, and affordability** and **addiction**).

Porn star

Someone who is famous for acting in porn films.

This is something of a misnomer. They are famous sometimes—but usually not rich. Most women and men in porn films don't make the big bucks that the word "star" would suggest, though they might become well known among the porn user crowd.

The best-known female porn actors usually make more money than the best-known male actors (see **woodsmen**), but they are subject to more physical and emotional abuse on the job (Faludi, 1999). While a few porn actors do well financially, most online sex actors do not make much money. A convenience sample of 134 female adult online sex performers found that fifty percent reported living in poverty in the last twelve months (Grudzen et al., 2011). Porn actors usually have no benefits and no retirement plans. Those who accept more abuse on the job earn more money but also experience more emotional and physical **trauma** (see **mental health** and **shorter lives**) (Braun, 2018; Maren, 2019).

Prostitution

An exchange of sex for money.

Online porn workers supply sexual imagery to **virtual johns**; they are **virtual prostitutes** who are paid for posing and performing sexually. Sometimes they have their own sites, and men pay subscription fees to access those sites. Other online sex models and actors are paid by the **virtual pimps** who run large porn sites. Ultimately, much of the money generated by the large porn sites comes from subscriptions to the sites or from companies that advertise on them (see **Big porn**, **boycott**, and **solutions** in the conclusion).

Obviously, the virtual john does not physically touch the online sex model. Nonetheless, there is an exchange of sex (or at least of sexual imagery) for money, which makes online sex acting a form of prostitution. A very few women who pose nude or semi-nude or who perform sex acts online become mainstream actors, models, or celebrities. This does not change the basic fact that they make sexual imagery available in exchange for payment. Hence, they are engaging in a type of prostitution.

It is important to note that most porn workers would not prostitute themselves if they had better opportunities. Eighty-nine percent of women who are in the sex business, online and off, say that they would prefer to do some other kind of work. Thus, helping young women get education and good jobs is an important way to limit the numbers who work in the sex industry (Grillo, 2020).

Pubic hair

Hair above and surrounding the genital area, which appears during puberty and signals sexual maturity.

As noted in the section on **evolutionary theory**, adult women and men normally have pubic hair. It indicates adulthood and a readiness to mate. Young children don't have pubic hair. The ubiquity in porn of women shaving or trimming their pubic hair or getting regular bikini waxes does not represent real life. It is yet another job requirement of online porn workers, time-consuming and, in the case of bikini waxes, **painful**. Concern about **pubic "five o'clock shadow"** is yet another unpleasant aspect of these jobs.

For the clueless porn user who has more experience with

porn than real women, a website called Make Love Not Porn offers a collection of helpful hints for men, including, "Some women shave (down there) and some women don't." Young men, many of whom are heavy porn users but less likely to have had actual **relationships**, are especially naïve in this regard (Twenge, 2017, p. 213).

If you are the partner of a porn user (or of a non-user who has picked up the view that the ideal woman is a hairless, or a near hairless, wonder "down there"), do not think that you have to shave or do bikini waxes. These are unpleasant procedures, and you have a right to the body you were born with—and a body that looks fully adult. Remember that you can also ask your partner to shave or wax *himself* and become a "hairless wonder" down there. His reaction may indicate a lot about his attitudes about women (see **entitlement**, **gender inequality**, **pain**, and **suffering**).

Public health

The science of promoting the conditions in which the physical and **mental health** of people and communities can flourish. Thus, public health is concerned about factors in the **environment** that make people sick or well and with the choices that will make a community of healthy people more likely.

Porn is increasingly recognized on the state level in the United States and in some other countries as a public health problem. It endangers lives and threatens relationships (see **divorce**). Porn has been likened to **smoking** (another public health hazard) and porn users to smokers (Eberstadt, 2009; Gobry, 2019). If you aren't a smoker yourself, would you want to date one? And if you aren't a porn user yourself, do you want to date or marry one?

Consider this:

"If porn made us healthy, we would be healthy by now." (Layden, n.d.)

Porn does not make people healthy. It is bad for their mental, emotional, and physical health. Public health advocates need to educate the public and government officials about it and help find **solutions** that will end the **porn pandemic** (Trueman & Rogers, 2019) (see **addiction**, **brain damage**, **erectile dysfunction**, **neuroscience**, **pain**, **PIED**, **pornified**, **shorter lives**, and **suffering**).

Pusher

A person, advertiser, or company that pressures people to do something that harms them, in this case, to do porn.

Porn changes and eventually injures the brain, causing addiction, harming **romantic relationships**, and creating large opportunity costs (i.e., there are many more positive things users could be doing with the time they spend viewing O-Mi's). As noted above, O-Mi's can be considered an addictive **drug**, and just as there are drug pushers, there are also porn pushers. The biggest pusher, of course, is **Big porn** itself.

Here are some examples of porn pushers. Porn sites send popups to men who have visited the site. **Virtual prostitutes** send texts with nude pictures attached, trying to get men to subscribe to their personal porn sites. Friends and family send porn; it functions to enhance male bonding, or they may send mostly innocuous articles of interest that have porn attached. They may do this to show that they are "with it" because they do porn, or maybe the author of the article attaches the porn to show how "masculine" and cool they are. Celebrities may pose nude or do sex scenes, often gratuitous to the main plot of the film or TV program, to advance their careers. They may do these scenes willingly, but it is important to keep in mind that film producers like Harvey Weinstein, now a convicted sex offender, may demand that an actor do these scenes. Selma Hayek recounts how Weinstein insisted on nudity and a sex scene with another woman when they were making *Frida*. He told her that if she didn't comply, he would shut down the film (see **bottom feeder films and TV programs**). Thus, Weinstein, not Hayek, is the pusher in this instance.

Of course, there is "push," and there is "pull." If men refused the stuff sent to them, they would stop getting so much of it. Someone trying to get clean from porn needs an excellent **porn blocker** and powerful ad and **spam** blockers. They need to block **XXX**, NC-17, and sexually focused NR films on their smart TVs. They also need to be gutsy enough to ask friends and family to stop sending them porn. They should not allow "cutesy" jokes about porn to be told in their presence (staying silent about porn jokes is similar to staying silent about racist jokes). In some future time, jokes about **Pornhub.com** will be considered as offensive as jokes about child murder.

Race inequality

The relative status and power of different races.

In contemporary societies, white people have higher status and power than brown and black peoples. Current racial stereotypes hold that whites deserve higher regard than nonwhites and a larger share of resources. The intersection of sex and race puts women of color at the bottom of the porn hierarchy. Porn perpetuates racial stereotypes. According to Pascal-Emmanuel Gobry (2019), "interracial porn not only has been getting more popular, and more degrading to women, but more racist."

A study by researchers at Indiana University Bloomington examined 1,741 scenes from two of the biggest online porn sites. Black women were more likely to be targets of aggression than white women, and black men were more likely to be sexually violent than white men. Scenes featuring Black couples were likely to depict aggression against women, more so than other racial pairings, including interracial couplings. The authors point out that these images teach behavior and habits (Porter, 2020).

It is typical for porn users and addicts to view material and have fantasies that are anathema to their core **values** (Weiss, 2013). One example is master-slave fantasies. **BDSM**, now common on most porn sites and in **XXX**, **NC-17**, and even R-rated films and TV-MA programs (see **bottom feeder films and TV programs**), often depicts this theme. The slave is usually, though not always, a female. It is important to recognize that the master-slave genre in pornography harkens back to the most brutal times in history and involves enacting inequality between the sexes and races. The porn user who is attached to this type of material has probably not examined whether it reflects his deeper values (see **recovery**) nor recognized the ugly historical roots of this material (see **gender inequality**, **hard-core**, **violence against women**, and **XXX**).

Rebooting

The process of moving from being addicted to porn to a **porn-free** state.

When a reboot is successful, the addict's brain and sexual functioning return to being normal for their age (see **brain injury**, **dopamine**, **neuroscience**, **recovery**, and **relapse**).

Recovery

"Learning to live a meaningful and comfortable life" without porn. Recovery is characterized by growth and the repair of past damage caused by the **addiction**.

Someone who is fully recovered reaches an understanding of what has happened to him and the injury that he has caused others (loved ones and performers in the sex industry) through his addiction (see **denial**). He has empathy for their suffering but also compassion for himself. He remains aware of the possibility of **relapse** even as he establishes a more fulfilling and balanced life. He knows that addiction rarely surrenders without a fight.

Terence Gorski (1989, pp. 3, 23) says that recovery is a lifelong journey and that the focus should be on maturation. The recovered addict will still have problems, but successfully managing them indicates movement toward the life they seek (Gorski, 1989, pp. 43, 44) (see **mature out**, **rebooting**, **solutions** in the conclusion, and **substitutions**).

Rehab

People with severe porn **addictions** may go to "rehab" (rehabilitation centers) to overcome their addiction. The addict will live with other addicts for weeks, or even months, in an environment where porn is not accessible and **triggers** are removed.

Psychologists and counselors will oversee their treatment. Addicts in rehab learn about their disease and about the tools available to become **porn-free**. Many, but not all, rehabilitation centers use **twelve-step** principles to help the addict move toward a healthier and happier life (see **mental health**, **recovery**, **solutions** in the conclusion, and **therapy**).

Relapse

Backsliding; slipping back into a former state. Relapse occurs when the O-Mi addict resumes their former porn habits.

Porn offers a level of stimulation far beyond what humans have evolved to handle. It is a "supernormal stimulant" (Wilson, 2017, p. 107). Small amounts of porn can alter the brain and behavior. According to Gary Wilson (2017, p. 107), significant negative effects can occur in the brain without the O-Mi viewer actually being addicted. Eventually, however, changes in the brain can lead to a constant craving for the next neurochemical rush and eventually to **addiction**. It will then be difficult to refrain from porn use given the many technologies available, the **environment**, and a culture that supports porn use. The man trying to reboot can easily relapse given these challenges (see **pornified**).

The addiction can continue indefinitely. As with any addiction, **recovery** typically involves a series of successes and setbacks (Maltz & Maltz, 2008, p. 186). Men who quit porn are said to be **rebooting**; they are attempting to return their brains and sexual functioning to their earlier **porn-free** state (see **brain injury** and **neuroscience**). To recover, it is important to avoid the **triggers** that initiate use and to find support through **therapy**, **twelve-step programs**, computer **porn blockers**, TV and movie service controls, and **accountability partners**. Having friends who don't view O-Mi's and an **oxytocin**-infused **love relationship** that includes mutual and loving support can also help prevent relapse.

The affordability of porn (see **AAA: The Triple A Engine of Porn**) makes recovery from porn addiction especially difficult. An alcoholic has to buy alcohol, and a smoker has to buy cigarettes or cigars, but a great deal of porn is free. Worse, as one addict attested, "the images feel burned into me" (Maltz

& Maltz, 2008, p. 188). That is, no external stimulus is even needed for the addiction to continue.

If porn addiction turns out to be similar to smoking and alcohol addictions, it may take five years of abstinence for remission to be considered reliably secure (Vaillant, 2012, p. 308). And if porn addiction is like smoking and alcoholism, the addict will not be able to safely return to **chipping** behaviors, but will need to stay consistently porn-free (Maltz & Maltz, 2008). There are many tools that can help them do this (see **solutions** in the conclusion).

Relationships

The caring human connections that some porn users risk losing as a result of their O-Mi viewing.

O-Mi viewers feel less relationship commitment than abstainers (Wilson, 2017, p. 24), and a **romantic** partner upset by the porn viewer's habit often feels less commitment to the user as well (see **divorce**). Porn use typically occurs in isolation, and as a porn habit deepens, the O-Mi viewer will feel less inclined to put in the time and effort needed for good relationships of all types. Porn users might not only lose romantic partners but might be disowned by their families and lose friendships.

Relationships are also central to **recovery** (see **intimacy**). A **porn-free environment** is important. To end a porn habit, it is essential to spend time with people who are not pro-porn and who discourage its use and to stay away from other users and addicts (see **pushers**). **Twelve-step** groups, however, are the exception to this latter point. While their members are users and addicts, the group exists to support all members in their quest to end their **addiction**.

It is not only people known to the porn user, however, who may influence his recovery. Studies of **smoking**, for example, indicate that smoking behavior extends to "three degrees of separation." This means that when one person quits smoking, it has a ripple effect not only on his friends but on his friends' friends and his friends' friends' friends (Christakis & Fowler, 2009, p. 116). Future network analysis may well show that O-Mi viewing and recovery have similar patterns.

Religion

Belief in and sense of connection to a higher power.

Porn is not a religious issue. People of all religious persuasions, agnostics, and atheists use porn. People of all religious persuasions, agnostics, and atheists are trying to quit. It is not the case, as some argue, that O-Mi viewing is mostly a problem for those who are religious (*Could Religious Expectations*, n.d.; Blythe, n.d.).

Research using representative samples shows, however, some relationships between religion and O-Mi viewing. Religion emphasizes **values** that can be critical for ending a porn habit. For example, religious people are less likely to use porn, yet they may be more likely to think that they have a porn **addiction** than other users; this is, perhaps, because they have values that are more clearly opposed to O-Mi viewing than irreligious people (Blythe, n.d.; Short et al., 2014).

For heavy porn users and porn addicts, the commitment and contemplation associated with spirituality and religion are supplanted by a "worship of porn" (Maltz & Maltz, p. 80). Most religions encourage **love** and selflessness, neither of which are found in porn and porn use.

My comments will reflect my Judeo-Christian background, though the views of many other religions are similar. Important values related to porn are covered in some of the ten commandments, which are examined below.

First, the porn user is worshiping false images: "sex goddesses" and other O-Mi images that cause a neurochemical rush (Chandra, 2012). In addition, they are coveting their neighbor's significant other or wife and committing adultery against their **romantic** partner, if they have one. The fantasies derived from O-Mi viewing have nothing to do with a user's partner. His **ogling** and fantasies also lead to masturbation that has nothing to do with his girlfriend or wife. We shouldn't be fooled because the neighbor's wife lives halfway around the world and is viewed on a television, computer screen, tablet, or phone (see **shock machines**). In the electronics era, we are a global village, and everyone is our neighbor.

Finally, the eighth commandment tells us not to lie, and in addition to coveting other people's mates and committing virtual or real adultery (which is associated with porn use, including **chipping**), most porn users are not truthful about what they are doing. O-Mi users usually don't want other people to know about their porn habits, so they lie in order to hide their behaviors (see **Dr. Jekyll and Mr. Hyde**, **dupes**, **secrets**, and **trust**). Lying and hiding are part of porn use and addiction, and the efforts required to cover up porn use make O-Mi viewing even more time-consuming. But on a positive note, lying and hiding also may indicate that the user or addict has more profound values than porn and knows that he is not living up to those values. These positive values, if followed, can lead him to a healthier and happier life (Peele, 2015).

Repression

Controlling or limiting expression of a psychological or social impulse.

Porn purveyors argue that they are battling repression. They claim that their goal is to liberate natural sexual desires

(Doidge, 2007, p. 102). Instead, they appear to be changing sexual proclivities, at least temporarily, given how plastic our brains are (see **fetishes**, **kink**, **neuroscience**, **secrets**, and **sexual deviance**).

We could as well argue that porn is emotional repression. Porn scripts rarely allow women and men to enact healthy attachments. The men in contemporary porn very often express hostility to the women, and the women appear self-hating, submissive, and masochistic in their acceptance of aggression and abuse (see **mental health**, **pain**, **suffering**, and **woodsmen**).

The viewers also exhibit emotional repression in that their sexual impulses are divorced from their feelings while they engage their porn habit, and their emotional attachments to girlfriends or wives are weakened by their porn habits (*Effects of Pornography on Marriage*, n.d.; Wilson, 2017) (see **divorce**, **intimacy**, **intimacy dysfunction**, **love**, **relationships**, and **romance**).

Reproductive success

Passing one's genes on to future generations.

The likelihood of reproductive success decreases as porn use increases (see **evolutionary theory**). Porn users may be less interested in having **relationships** with real people, may develop **erectile dysfunction** at relatively young ages (see **PIED**), may marry later or not at all (Twenge, 2017), and might be more likely to have offspring with physical or mental defects (due to conceiving children at older ages). It thus appears that porn is anti-reproduction. Rather than increasing reproductive success, it probably decreases it. From an evolutionary perspective, porn could be said to be one big joke on humanity (see **intercourse** and **sex recession**).

Romance

The feelings and behavior of two people who are in love; a **love** affair.

Though romance is valued in Western cultures, it is important to note that not all societies share this **value**. Many societies have arranged marriages. It was only in the 12th century that a focus on romance emerged in Europe, and then only between a married woman and an unmarried man. These romances were expected to fail. Nonetheless, it is important to discuss here because romance is currently highly valued in Western culture, as can be seen in our mainstream (non-porn) movies and music (Doidge, 2007, p. 96).

Porn is not about **love** or romance, except in some users' fantasies (see **defenses, psychological**). The user would almost never be able to attract the women that they are **ogling**. People in actual relationships are usually similar in age and physical attractiveness (except perhaps when the male is wealthy) (Christakis & Fowler, 2009, p. 70). This is often not true of the porn viewer and the O-Mi's on their screens. Sex models and performers are usually **cyborg femmes**, and their good looks will typically surpass those of the porn viewer. They will also often be younger than the viewer. In the meantime, the porn user's real-life partner, if they have one, generally feels less romantic toward them because of their O-Mi viewing. As noted earlier, porn kills sex (Wilson, 2017, p. 6). It also kills romance (see **chick repellent**, **divorce**, **fear of aging**, **intimacy**, and **love**).

Secrets

Most porn users try to keep their behavior a secret, especially from their **romantic** partner and children, if they have them. They might share O-Mi's with their friends, however, in a spirit of male comradery.

Secret-keeping, however, is not healthy behavior. One of the slogans from Alcoholics Anonymous, also used by other **twelve-step** groups, is "you're only as sick as your secrets" (Andriote, 2018). Secrets preclude **intimacy** and closeness in a romantic relationship. The romantic partner feels like a **dupe** when they discover their mate masturbating to porn or their O-Mi stash (see **fapper**, **love**, **musterbater**, **relationship**, **romance**, and **shock machines**)—and they are a dupe. A porn user's secret destroys **trust**. Once discovered, he is likely to lose (even now, in this **porn pandemic**) the respect of many of the people in his circle, and in some instances, even his family and job (see **Dr. Jekyll and Mr. Hyde**).

Sex Addicts Anonymous (SAA)

A **twelve-step** group for people with sex **addictions**, including porn addictions. Membership is open to anyone who is trying to end their sex addiction.

The fellowship tries to help members explore what healthy sexuality means to them with the guidance of their higher power. There are a variety of similar groups but this is one of the best known. The groups follow many of the guidelines set up by Alcoholics Anonymous, which was the original twelve-step group (see **religion**).[6]

Sex addiction

The **compulsion** to have a certain type of sex.

There are many kinds of sex addictions. A craving for porn is one type, but O-Mi **addiction** is often, but not always, connected with other addictions. Some online porn users visit

---

6 The website for Hope and Freedom Counseling Services has an extensive list of treatment resources. See "More Sex Addiction Resources," Hope & Freedom, accessed September 18, 2021, https://www.hopeandfreedom.com/more-treatment-resources.

sexual chat rooms, have sex with real-life **prostitutes**, or meet up with nonvirtual women to commit adultery.

Sex recession

The phenomenon of people having less sex than in the past.

There are likely multiple reasons for this change. It is also true that this phenomenon may be overhyped (Reese, 2019). In the context of this book, however, it is worth noting that some commentators argue that the viewing of OMi's leads some people to have less sex with real-life partners (Regnerus & Uecker, 2011, p. 96; Wilcox & Stone, 2019) (see **iGen**).

Twenge suggests that porn probably does not decrease sexual activity, yet "there appears to be a measurable segment of people for whom porn is enough and real sex seems unnecessary. Why risk rejection, **sexually transmitted diseases**, **relationship** arguments, or having to meet up with someone when you can watch in the privacy of your bedroom and do things your way?" (Twenge, 2017, p. 213).

Sexual deviance

Sexual behaviors that are regarded as atypical or immoral by most people in a specific culture or historical period. Sexual deviance is sometimes referred to as "**weird sex**."

Many of the paraphilias depicted in the online sex world are practiced by only a small number of people. These behaviors may be considered morally questionable or objectionable even by those who regularly view them online (and even by some who practice them). Most people who experiment with these sexual behaviors find that their physical, emotional, or spiritual discomfort with them makes the experimentation short-lived (Regnerus & Uecker, 2011, p. 94).

Make-believe (role-playing) aggression and violence are common in porn, but some of what is depicted causes real bodily and mental harm. **BDSM** continues to be stigmatized by much of society because the real or pseudo-aggression that it entails, even when consensual, is seen as unacceptable and sexually deviant by many people (see **violence against women**). Other kinds of **kink** also continue to conflict with the **values** of much of the population (see **fetishes**), even the values of some O-Mi users who are viewing it online.

Compared to past generations of youth, younger people may have a lower frequency of sexual activity with actual partners (see **iGen** and **sex recession**). This might be partly due to the fact that some are regularly titillated by practices online that some of them consider sexually deviant—but they don't want to enact inegalitarian, aggressive, and "cruel" sex themselves (Twenge, 2017, p. 213) (see **gender inequality**, **hard-core**, **racial inequality**, and **XXX**).

Sexual healing

The emotional and physical benefits of loving sex.

Intimate sexual connection enhances our immune systems and supports or improves our health. Furthermore, our bodies, our immunity, and our mental and physical well-being are "intimately connected with the world around us" (Pearsall, 1994, p. 36). Thus, the physical, cultural, and emotional facets of our **environments** have a large impact on our health.

The **porn pandemic** is occurring in an environment that is unhealthy for everyone in it—and we are all now affected because the porn industry (see **Big porn** and **pushers**) is wide-reaching and has tentacles that reach into everyday life. Here's a thought-provoking quote from one of Pearsall's patients:

It's like we are alone in our skin-mobiles, driving along alone through life. Sometimes we have an accident and make a connection with someone else, but we get hurt because we don't know how to connect safely. (1994, p. 39)

Pearsall makes clear that intimacy requires *skills* that can only be honed through **relationships**. These skills cannot be acquired through viewing porn.

Sexually transmitted diseases (STDs)

Infections that are passed from one person to another via vaginal, oral, or anal sex.

Online porn workers contract these illnesses at alarmingly high rates while performing sexually for the public. Though the porn industry uses a nationwide program called PASS (Performer Availability Screening Services), and porn actors are tested every 14 days for HIV and other STDs, the risk is inherent to the job.

In addition, some O-Mi users seek out casual real-life partners and are at risk of STD infections as a result. If they are in a **romantic relationship**, their wife or girlfriend is at risk as well. (Grudzen & Kerndt, 2007; Grudzen et al., 2009; Hollow, 2020).

Sexy vs. sexual

Looking desirable vs. having a strong sexual drive and response.

These are not the same thing. Online sex models and actors often spend significant amounts of time and money to make themselves appear as sexy and desirable as possible, to attract a larger audience. Ironically, some of these efforts can diminish sexual response. Fake breasts, for example, have less nipple sensation and less erotic sensitivity than breasts without implants (Newman, 2017). They will also often feel cold to both the woman and to her sexual partners (Breastcancer.org Community, 2014) (see **beautiful women**, **cyborg femmes**, **female breast mutilation**, and **female genital mutilation**).

Shock machines

Electronic devices used to view pornography. They may contain saved O-Mi's—i.e., the harem and sex film collections of the porn user. Devices include computers, phones, tablets, and smart TVs.

The partner and the children of the O-Mi viewer will be shocked if they find this porn or see the porn user viewing these sexual images. Phones, tablets, and laptops may even be used for that purpose in public. Complaints about men viewing porn on airplanes, for example, are increasing (Miller, 2018).

A man who wants to leave his porn habit behind will need to clean up his shock machines. This may take considerable effort, but if he doesn't do this, blocking new porn will be to no avail because his past collections will still be available to him (see **bottom feeder films and TV programs** and **porn blockers**).

Shorter lives

Premature death.

Early death appears to be a risk for porn workers. Many go into the business thinking that they can limit their online sexual activities, and then they find out they cannot. Many get out of the business within a few months (Faludi, 1999, pp. 546, 547), but those who stay are at risk.

PTSD (post-traumatic stress disorder) is common among female porn workers. A number of the women on **Pornhub.com**, a major porn site, are deceased. They have committed suicide or died of **drug** overdoses or in accidents that are suspicious (Maren, 2018) (see **mental health**).

Users may think that O-Mi viewing will keep them "young" (see **Dr. Jekyll and Mr. Hyde** and **fear of aging**), but they might live shorter lives if they end up **divorced** because of pornography use. Married men have a longevity advantage over both never married and divorced men (*Marriage and Men's Health*, 2019; Thompson, 2019). Never married and divorced men lack the substantial emotional and physical support that many wives provide to their husbands. The **sexual healing** and **intimacy** of which Paul Pearsall writes are not available to men without **romantic** partners, though other kinds of intimacy are and may also contribute to longevity (Casciotti & Zuckerman, n.d.). It is likely that men who live with a **romantic** partner but who are not married, gain many of the health protections available to married men. Statisticians should calculate the excess male mortality caused by porn use, divorce, never-married status, and the increased loneliness that results.

On the other hand, divorce does not reduce the longevity of women nearly as much. It is likely that, on average, men do not support their wives as much as wives support their husbands. Women who divorce porn addicts probably enhance their physical and mental health and, perhaps, improve their longevity. Besides determining mortality statistics on males as indicated above, our understanding of the effects of porn would be enhanced if we had mortality statistics comparing women married to (a) porn addicts, (b) recovered porn addicts, and (c) men who don't do porn (who, admittedly, are increasingly hard to find because of the **porn pandemic**).

Smoking

Inhalation of the smoke of burning tobacco, which when done regularly becomes an **addiction** with negative health effects. The brain changes caused by this addiction are similar to those caused by porn addiction.

O-Mi viewing is frequently compared to smoking, and anti-porn activists often say that "porn is the new smoking" (*Does the Porn Industry Use Tobacco Tactics?* 2018; Eberstadt, 2009). As noted, both smoking and O-Mi viewing are addicting. Both reduce the attractiveness of the user to others. Both are huge industries, referred to as Big Tobacco and **Big porn**. Both can negatively affect the addict's life, including less robust health and **shorter lives** (Gobry, 2019).

The experience of **relapse** may also be similar for porn addicts and smokers. Mark Twain is said to have stated that quitting smoking was so easy that he did it hundreds of times. Quitting porn may well be so easy that the user or addict quits numerous (but hopefully not hundreds) of times before being able to stop for good.

The following cartoon could be altered to reflect a porn viewer's activities*:

Fig. 1. *Change to: "If I can't even control my hand to put down my penis... How will I ever do anything in life?" (*Graphic courtesy of https://lifeclub.org/*)

Soft-core

Porn that depicts nude or nearly nude women and men and sexual activities that are not aggressive or violent.

Soft-core porn may depict sexual intercourse, for example, which in the past was considered to be **hard-core** porn, but which now is considered "tame" and soft-core. Gobrey (2019) argues that while soft-core pornography can still be found, most porn now fuses **violence against women** and sex. Using the definitions in this book, that indicates that the majority of porn is now hard-core. Research suggests that even soft-core porn leads to greater acceptance of **violence against women**, perhaps, because women are still objectified, and the viewer sees them as less than human (see **objects**). Studies show that the "future likelihood of raping a woman" is correlated with soft-core as well as hard-core porn use. Both soft-core and hard-core porn viewing are correlated with using verbal pressure, alcohol, and drugs to coerce sexual activity. Porn's effect depends on the frequency of exposure as well as on the type of porn viewed. More frequent viewing of any type of O-Mi's is associated with a greater likelihood of sexual coercion (Layden, 2010, pp. 62-63) (see **solutions** in the conclusion).

Spam

Spam consists of unsolicited email and text messages. The spam sender thus "trespasses" on the receiver's electronic property.

Many men receive a daily barrage of porn spam. Someone who is trying to become **porn-free** and has a **porn blocker** on his computer, tablet, and phone, and movie and TV controls that block overly sexy shows (see **bottom feeder films and TV shows**) might still be unable to avoid spam with nude or semi-nude images and come-hither messages. The **pusher** might be a porn site or an individual woman trying to get him to subscribe to her personal site. Porn spam is similar to a woman wearing a coat showing up at one's door, then opening the coat to show that she's nude or scantily clad.

Spam blockers send unsolicited emails and text messages to a spam folder, but the messages remain on the electronic device until they are deleted. They are, thus, another danger to O-Mi users who are trying to become porn-free.

Spam is illegal in the U.K. Unsolicited marketing emails may not be sent to individuals, though relevant emails may be sent to corporate entities if they are related to their work. There are hefty fines for those who break the law (*Is Spamming Illegal in the UK?* 2020). Other countries could enact similar laws, which would greatly reduce or eliminate spam, including porn spam.

Sports Illustrated Swimsuit Issue

A yearly issue of ***Sports Illustrated*** that features women wearing barely-there swimsuits or only paint.

This issue has been published every February since 1964. The women are models, celebrities, and athletes wearing tiny bikinis or painted on "swimsuits." Their attire can be pasties and a string. The question of whether this is porn is irrelevant since, as noted earlier, there is no agreed-upon definition of porn. The pictures are certainly O-Mi's—**o**gle **m**asturbatory **i**mages. They are used for **ogling** and masturbation. Ogling is not good for the ogler, who is objectifying women and sees them as less than human as a result (see **objects** above). The women get paid, but they become part of an industry that has negative impacts on women and men alike (Heflick, 2014).

Stinking thinking

Any thinking that might lead a **recovering** or recovered addict back to porn use (see **relapse**). A term originally used in Alcoholics Anonymous, but which can apply to any **addiction**, including porn addiction (Weiss, 2013).

Here are some examples: The porn user thinks that he really does not have a problem (**denial**) or just a minor one that will not interfere with his **relationships** or life. He thinks that he can **ogle** women in swimsuits for just a little while and not **trigger** a desire to look longer or at more explicit pictures. Or he thinks that pausing his smart TV to ogle the near-nude or (occasionally) nude women depicted in some R movies (see **bottomfeeder films and TV programs**) won't cause cravings or create an urge to go on internet searches to get a continued fix.

Over time the term has come to cover all critical, disapproving dialogue in an addict's brain (Milos, 2019). This might include thoughts such as: "I am unlovable, and I don't deserve better," and "My situation is hopeless, and there is no way out of my addiction."

Substitution

Replacing porn viewing with other activities that produce a neurochemical high.

There are poor substitutes and good substitutes. A poor substitute is the continued viewing of O-Mi's, just in a less extreme form. The viewer who has been focused on **violence against women** now shifts his attention to nude females. If he has been addicted to pictures of nude women, he starts **ogling** women in the ***Sports Illustrated Swimsuit Issue***. He might watch raunchy R movies rather than **XXX** films or regularly view sexed-up TV-MA programs to get his fix (see **bottom feeder films and TV programs**). While this kind of substitution can represent progress, it is nonetheless a danger to **recovery** (Wilson, 2017, pp. 156-157).

Other substitutes do not include O-Mi viewing but are still in the "poor" category because they undermine the addict's mental or physical health. Possibilities are gambling, compulsive eating, **smoking**, and candy binges. In Vaillant's (2012, pp. 312–313) study, some alcohol abusers replaced alcohol with marijuana, a substitute that might be seen as positive or negative depending on one's **values** and on how it is used.

A good substitute will reflect the user's more transcendent **values**. These substitutes include meaningful work or hobbies that engage the person's interests and allow for the use of his talent(s) (see **environment**). Helping others might be a positive substitute (see **twelve-step programs**), as could an **oxytocin**-based **romantic relationship** (Love, 2016). Maltz and Maltz (2008, p. 232), sex counselors and authors of *The Porn Trap*, suggest that "**intimacy**-oriented sex" provides a way to combine the positive feelings the porn user has about himself and a current or future partner with "sexual desire, arousal, and orgasm…It honors conditions of healthy sexuality, such as responsibility, respect, and caring."

Suffering

Unpleasant physical or emotional sensations.

Many sex performers endure physical and emotional abuse when they participate in porn shoots. They are also at substantial risk for **sexually transmitted diseases**. In addition, they undergo various uncomfortable, unhealthy, and painful procedures in order to work in the sex field. Eighty-five percent of online female sex models and actors have breast implants (Maltz & Maltz, 2008), and some endure genital surgeries (see **female breast mutilation** and **female genital mutilation**). Many female performers wax their **pubic** and other hair (no joke: this is a painful process). Males may wax their chest hair. Excessive dieting and exercise are common risks for both female and male online sex models and performers (Grudzen et al., 2009).

Male porn users sometimes ask girlfriends and wives to mimic the look of female porn workers: more suffering. Awareness of a male partner's O-Mi viewing can cause unease, distrust, and trauma. **Romantic** partners often find themselves in a **relationship** with unsatisfactory sex or no sex at all (Paul, 2005).

Users of porn may develop **erectile dysfunction** from frequent O-Mi viewing (**PIED**). Their mental health is often subpar, and they may be on multiple medications for depression, anxiety, and stress disorders. A serious porn habit may cause them to lose relationships and jobs (see **BDSM**, **divorce**, **fetishes**, **gender inequality**, **kink**, **mental health**, **pain**, **racial inequality**, **sexual deviance**, **shorter lives**, **violence against women**, and **XXX**).

Therapy

Treatment to help someone recover from physical, mental, and emotional disease or injury.

Porn **addiction** is a chronic brain disease that involves injury to the neurological system (see **brain damage**, **erectile dysfunction**, **neuroscience**, and **PIED**). Patrick Carnes, an expert in sex addiction, says the neuroscience of addiction is now "very, very clear" (Smith, 2019, p. 2). This injury can be at least partly reversed by abstention from porn (see **rebooting**). Many people find therapy helps them progress toward this goal.

While seeing a counselor or therapist can be an important part of discontinuing a porn habit or addiction, not just any therapist will do. Many therapists have their own porn habits or addictions and see nothing wrong with viewing O-Mi's. They may have a libertine stance toward porn, or they may hold the old view that O-Mi's are a marital aid. Nothing could be further from the truth for most couples, at least in the long term.

While therapists with a variety of backgrounds and treatment orientations can benefit the porn addict, to be helpful, they must take porn addiction seriously (which many psychologists and psychiatrists do not). They also need to hold the addict **accountable**; a therapist who is tough and refuses to work with an addict who doesn't make progress is better than one who lets him continue his habit so that they can retain him as a client (Smith, 2019, p. 6).

In some cases, it may be useful to find a therapist who has experienced their own porn addiction and is working to overcome it. These therapists will have especially deep understandings of the challenges that the addict faces (Littlejohn, 2009, p. 147) (see **solutions** in the conclusion). Counselors and psychologists can help the O-Mi addict reclaim a healthier and happier life.

While therapy is essential to the **recovery** of many porn addicts (Smith, 2019), it is not always critical. Returning to their healthier and more supportive home **environments** was enough incentive for most Vietnam veterans to quit their drug habits. Sometimes even **willpower** is enough to overcome addiction (Peele, 2004, p. 107).

Three-Second rule

A technique that helps the O-Mi viewer defuse **triggers** and practice **eye bounce**. The porn user turns away from a triggering image within three seconds.

He does not take another look, but instead, he thinks about the female(s) in the image as someone's daughter, sister, or wife, and then mentally sends that individual and their family his sincere best wishes (Brassart, 2020) (see **ogling**).

Tough love

Strict but kind treatment of someone as a way of helping them overcome a problem. Refusing to **enable** a bad habit or addiction.

Protecting a **love** affair or marriage may require an attitude of "**zero tolerance**" toward porn. An alcoholic cannot drink and avoid abusing alcohol in the long term (Vaillant, 2012, p. 359), and O-Mi addicts cannot view porn or engage in **chipping** if they want to avoid **relapse**. Maltz and Maltz (2008, p. 257) suggest that porn addicts "must avoid porn for the rest of their lives."

Porn users usually want their partners to keep loving them, but "tough love" is necessary if the **romantic** partner does not want porn to affect their **relationship** (see **cheating**, **chipping**, **divorce**, **erectile dysfunction**, **mental infidelity**, and **PIED**). Partners should not assume that they have to put up with a user's porn habit.

Not only can a partner who shows tough love to their porn-using mate help them quit, so can a therapist who shows tough love to a porn-using client. Dr. Patrick Carnes suggests some of the best sex **addiction** therapists are the toughest. They hold patients **accountable** and refuse to treat patients who don't make progress under their care (and refer them to another therapist) (Smith, 2019, p. 6).

Trafficking

Criminal activity that uses force and coercion to lure females (and a smaller number of males) into sexual exploitation. Some of the victims are minors (see **legal**).

Some porn actors on O-Mi sites may have been kidnapped, transported against their will, and forced into porn work. It is impossible to know how common this **modern-day slavery** is, but, as noted earlier, we should be especially concerned about the so-called "teen" sites (see **legal**). The porn user may argue that all the teens on those sites are at least 18 and legal or that the women are really older and are there of their own volition. But how does anyone know? They often look, and perhaps are, much younger than 18. **Pornhub.com** (one of the biggest and best-known sites) does not have contracts with the sex models and actors on their site; consequently, the performers have little legal protection (Trafficking Hub, n.d.).

Because of ongoing negative publicity and **lawsuits** brought against the site and its executives, Pornhub.com deleted over 75 percent of its sex films in December 2020. If one of the best-known sites does not have safeguards in place, it is likely that the problem exists on other sites as well. **The National Center against Sexual Exploitation** is aiding trafficked girls and women, sex performers who have no contracts, and those whose contracts have been ignored by porn purveyors (Oss, 2020).

Trigger

Things in a person's **environment** or in their internal emotional or physical feelings that cause a craving for porn.

External triggers include "being around sexually provocative people and contact with porn delivery systems such as the internet and cable TV. Common internal triggers include feeling stressed, upset, lonely, angry, depressed, anxious, run-down, sexually frustrated, or being under the influence of alcohol or drugs" (Maltz & Maltz, 2008) (see **H.A.L.T.**). Some men may be triggered by sitting in the chair where they have viewed O-Mi's in the past or by being on the beach surrounded by women in skimpy swimsuits. A common trigger is finding oneself alone in an apartment or house; the closing door when other occupants leave is a trigger. Others may be triggered by R-rated movies. **R** equals **R**aunchy in many films, which can contain a considerable amount of sexual material and nudity. They are often a trigger, sending some men on O-Mi hunting expeditions, or they are in and of themselves a minor porn source. Some addicts consciously use the media to trigger cravings (see **bottom feeder films and TV programs**).

In general, sexy clothing, sexual scenes, nudity, and semi-nudity are external triggers, and negative emotions are internal triggers. Triggers are specific to the individual, however, and some men are triggered by things that others would find surprising—stuff that "isn't that bad." A Fight the New Drug release puts it this way:

> You know the stuff we're talking about here: shows, movies or games that feature content that isn't necessarily pornographic but is just the right amount of suggestive. We get that these things can be really entertaining, but you need to ask yourself, is it worth it? Don't jeopardize your **recovery** for something as common as a trashy reality TV show or rated M video game. Basically, just be honest with yourself. Some people will have personal triggers that have nothing to do with explicit content. For example...

> *I used to justify looking at porn by saying if it wasn't real people, it was ok, so I would search for drawn or animated stuff. This led me to find things that featured characters from my favorite shows and games. Now, those games are huge triggers for me. It sucks but I have to stay away from them now.* -Ryan, 25 (4 Triggers that Are Slipping Under Your Radar, n.d.)

To the porn viewer who is trying to end his habit: If you are serious about stopping your porn habit, you will avoid all the triggers that have caused you to view O-Mi's in the past. You will also avoid **pushers**, who include anyone who encourages you to use porn, including advertisers, coworkers, friends, and family members. The material they send can trigger cravings and **relapse** (Amen & Smith, 2010). You have to be ready to push back and reject whatever may interfere with your **recovery**.

Triple A engine

See **AAA: accessibility, anonymity, and affordability**.

Trust

Confidence in the truthfulness and integrity of another person.

When we trust, we believe that the other person will not lie to us and that we can fully know them. Since porn users and addicts fib and hide their activities to ensure that they can maintain their habits without being challenged, it becomes hard for partners and other family members to trust them (see **Dr. Jekyll and Mr. Hyde**, **dupes**, and **secrets**).

Anger can be a way to hide one's activities. If a user or addict yells or otherwise acts aggressively when questioned, it will be difficult to ask him about his activities. Anger, in short, can be a warning sign and should cause family members and **accountability partners** to be concerned about whether the anger is hiding dishonesty.

Being in active treatment can help restore trust. Promises are not sufficient; a more active stance must be taken for the O-Mi viewer to regain the trust of their partner (and family). It is unlikely that **willpower**, even in the best-intentioned person, will be adequate to end a porn habit or **addiction** (see **solutions** in the conclusion).

Trust is not all or nothing. A **romantic** partner may come to trust a porn user boyfriend or husband more as he strives to minimize his viewing of O-Mi's and become a **porn-free guy**. Or she may trust him less and less if she sees evidence of his porn habit deepening and eating up more of his time and sexual energy. Trust thus exists on a continuum.

Everyone who has a romantic partner hopes to be able to trust them fully, but trust must be earned. For full **recovery** and health, the porn addict's hiding and lying need to stop. Only then can trust be restored (Smith, 2019).

Twelve-step programs

Groups comprised of members who help each other recover from **addiction**, typically led by a therapist.

In the case of sex addictions, including porn addictions, the therapist oversees discussions focusing on members' sexual experiences and on pertinent educational materials. In a twelve-step program, users give up their lives to a higher power, however they may define it. The message twelve-step groups have for their members is that "selfishness" and "self-centeredness" are the root of their addiction problem. They allow the addict to get honest feedback from others who share their experiences. (Littlejohn, 2009, pp 147-8) (see **religion**, **Sex Addicts Anonymous (SAA),** and **values**).

Twelve-step groups for porn addicts include **Sex Addicts Anonymous (SAA)**, Sexaholics Anonymous (SA), Sex and Love Addicts Anonymous (SLAA), Sexual Compulsives Anonymous (SCA), and Sexual Recovery Anonymous (SRA). Twelve-step groups for **romantic** partners include **Infidelity Survivors Anonymous (ISA)** and S-Anon. There are others, but these are some of the most well-known groups (*More Sex Addiction Treatment Resources*, n.d.).

George Vaillant (2012, p. 314) suggests that helping others toward **recovery** is critical in overcoming addiction. He writes this about Alcoholics Anonymous, which is a twelve-step program: "AA is as much about self-help as a barn-raising. In both of these community activities, success is at least as much about helping other people as about helping yourself."

Vagina

The tube between the vulva and the cervix. In penile-vaginal **intercourse**, the man moves his penis in and out of the vagina or (if the woman is on top), her vagina is around the penis, and she moves so that it goes in and out.

Vaginas hold less interest for men now that they have porn. Many would rather view O-Mi's than have sex with a flesh and blood woman. Women who want **relationships** thus have a harder time establishing them (**sex recession**).

Naomi Wolf has said that vaginas "used to have a pretty high exchange value." Getting into a relationship with a woman was special (Regnerus & Ueckers, 2011, p. 99). Now many men see a real woman's vagina as being boring compared to those of the **cyborg femmes**, many of whom lack **pubic hair** (and look like a little girl "down there") and whose vaginas sometimes are surgically altered to be "neat and tidy" (Kirkman, 2019; Creighton, 2014). A significant number of men become fixated on watching anal sex online and some of them pressure the women in their lives to have this kind of sex, though it appears that most women (and many men) don't find it that pleasurable (Wilson, 2017, p. 181)

Values

Fundamental beliefs that guide action. Examples are truth, goodness, and health.

Finding ways to reconnect with one's deepest values is

essential for someone who wants to end their porn use or **addiction** (Peele, 2015). Most people, including O-Mi viewers, think that **love**, kindness, and decency are important to a fulfilling life, but porn users' online behavior belies these values. As noted earlier, they are **Dr. Jekyll**—but also **Mr. Hyde**. Porn users are often "nice guys," yet their desires and sense of **entitlement** lead them to **objectify** women. In their worst guise, they seek out images of physical and verbal abuse of women to get a sexual high. There may be a dissociation of their two sides (Griffin-Shelley, 1995) (see **gender inequality**, **hard-core**, **racial inequality**, **violence against women**, and **XXX**).

Paul Pearsall suggests that values can help people make choices that favor **intimacy**, **sexual healing**, and health (see **erectile dysfunction**, **mental health**, **PIED**, and **shorter lives**). At times, following one's values may need to override physical impulses in order to protect **relationships** and to ensure the emotional, mental, and physical health of the **recovering** O-Mi user and his **romantic** partner, if he has one (Pearsall, 1994, p. 126). Humane values also lessen the demand for porn and, in the big picture, protect porn industry workers (see **solutions** in the conclusion: porn performers would benefit greatly if more education and job opportunities were available to them.)

Violence against women

The use of physical force to cause pain, injure, or kill a female. If the woman is murdered, it is **femicide**.

Desire for this type of material is widespread, and porn users can easily access violent scenes on porn sites. Studies vary in their conclusions about the degree of violence in porn films, but it is high. A study of **Pornhub.com** and Xvideos.com found that 45 percent of the videos on Pornhub.com and 35 percent of those on Xvideos.com portrayed violence or aggression, almost all of it against women (Fritz et al., 2020). Other studies find even higher rates of violence: a content analysis of the fifty top-selling porn movies found that 88 percent showed physical aggression toward women, primarily gagging, spanking, and slapping (Bridges et al., 2010) (see **hard-core** and **XXX**).

The longer a man uses online porn, the more likely he might be to seek violent porn in which women are the victims. Dr. Norman Doidge (2013) writes that "as tolerance for excitement develops it no longer satisfies; only by releasing a second drive, the aggressive drive, can an addict be excited." According to **neuroscientists**, viewing aggressive and violent porn desensitizes the viewer to images that would have offended him when he was **porn-free**. Whether these desensitized men are more likely to be violent against women in their offline lives remains a contested issue. A 2015 literature review found 22 studies from seven different countries showing a link between viewing online porn and sexual aggression (Gobry, 2019). Even men who view porn that is not violent show a greater tolerance of violence against women when compared to **porn-free** men (see **soft-core**) (Layden, 2010, pp. 62-63).

Virtual john

A male who goes online to view O-Mi's.

The porn user might or might not pay directly for this material. Some have subscriptions to a woman's individual site and, hence, pay her directly. Some pay for subscriptions to sites like **Pornhub.com**; if they pay more, they can get "content" without ads. Others seek out sites that make porn available for free; the sites generate funds through advertisements. In the latter two cases, the **virtual prostitute** may be paid by the **virtual pimps** who run the site (see **john** and **voyeur**). Some of the women on these sites, however, are not virtual prostitutes. Instead, they have been **trafficked** in which case they are likely to receive no pay and have their images uploaded without their permission. The virtual john cannot be sure that all the images that he views are **legal**. However, it is certain that the virtual pimps will earn money from the images, legal or not.

Virtual pimps

The people (mostly men) who run the online porn industry sites.

Their goal is to make money, though they may donate to causes like environmentalism. They try to come off as good guys ensuring everyone's sexual **freedom**. Instead, their work furthers sexual and **relationship** dysfunctions (see **cheating**, **chipping**, **divorce**, **erectile dysfunction**, **mental infidelity**, **PIED**, **repression**, and **shorter lives**) and the view that women are less human than men (see **objects**). Some of them are involved in **trafficking** (see **Pornhub.com**), and to the extent that some of their activities may be illegal, they are subject to **lawsuits** and criminal prosecution.

Virtual prostitutes

The women (and men) who model and act in online porn. Women who used to work as virtual prostitutes or in other types of prostitution are sometimes referred to as **survivors**.

Porn workers may or may not receive money directly from the **virtual john**. Some have their own sites to which an O-Mi viewer subscribes. Others are paid by **virtual pimps** who oversee large sites like **Pornhub.com** (see **Big porn**); these sites generate funds through subscriptions or through advertisements that companies pay to put on the sites.

If a woman works for virtual pimps, she may or may not avoid the damage inflicted on prostitutes who have physical sex with **johns**. Both the producers of porn and online male sex partners may be abusive. The more rough sex and **violence** the sex performer allows, the more she will earn—but the more likely she will develop PTSD, a **drug** habit, and poor **mental health**. The ultimate risk is that she may die at a relatively young age (see **shorter lives**).

In an interview with Elly Arrow (2020), Luba Fein, an Israeli activist working against **prostitution**, says that the situation of virtual prostitutes is worse than that of offline prostitutes: "They suffer so much more. They weren't just coerced into paid rape... they cope their entire life with the feeling of being watched. Their abuse is documented. It is distributed." In speaking of the particular case of a woman who had been a porn actor, she says, "when she is going to the mall or just walking down the street... She can never feel safe because she fears that people recognize her."

Offline prostitution takes place in a specific locale (though for a variety of reasons, including sex **trafficking**, not necessarily in the prostitute's area of origin), but online prostitution is available to men across the globe on the internet. Hence, the feeling of virtual prostitutes that they can never escape from their online work, no matter that they have exited that work and built new lives.

There are many reasons that women end up working in porn. Some of them are shown in Figure 2.

Fig. 2. Reasons women work in porn (*Graphic courtesy of* https://www.iamatreasure.com)

If you are a porn worker who wants to get out of the industry, there is help. See **https://fightthenewdrug.org/if-youre-in-the-sex-industry-and-youre-thinking-of-leaving-harmony-dust-grillo/**

Also see **https://www.iamatreasure.com/**

Voyeur

Someone who enjoys looking at nudity and semi-nudity and sexual acts but does not then participate in sex with the people that he is viewing (see **virtual john**).

The popularity of internet porn may mean that we are creating a world where voyeurism is on the rise, but other, more active sexuality with real-life partners is on the decrease (see **erectile dysfunction**, **intercourse**, **PIED**, and **sex recession**). According to Maltz and Maltz (2008, p. 21), authors of *The Porn Trap*, voyeurs "have the upper hand in a relationship because, while they have the prerogative of critiquing, judging and—with the simple click of a mouse—rejecting someone else, they don't have to suffer being similarly scrutinized or sexually snubbed."

VPNs

A virtual private network, available for free or by subscription. An example is Express VPN.

VPNs are a common way to ensure that the VPN user cannot be blocked from using porn. In short, VPNs block **porn-blocking programs**. VPNs also speed up internet service. Nonetheless, their ability to block porn blocking programs means that anyone trying to give up porn should not use one.

Knowledge of VPNs is **essential** for **accountability partners**. They will not be effective in that role if they are not vigilant about the O-Mi viewer's VPN use. If the user or addict is using a

VPN, their O-Mi viewing will be invisible to the porn blocking program and to the accountability partner. The partner will then be less able to help the user overcome their porn habit. The partner should also beware of browsers that are also VPNs.

Willpower

The ability to control one's own thoughts and behavior.

For those wanting to kick a porn habit or **addiction**, consciously acting to avoid sexual images will usually not be enough, at least in the longer term. Willpower is a relatively exhausting effort. Many people drastically underestimate the likelihood of backsliding, which is huge (Wood, 2019). For most users, a program that blocks porn on their electronic devices, content controls on their smart TVs that block **XXX**, NC-17, and sexually focused NR films (see **bottom feeder films and TV programs**), an **accountability partner**, **therapy**, and a **twelve-step program** will be helpful. **Porn blocker** programs and smart TV controls ensure that the user doesn't have to exert mental control; the program or control setting does it for them. An accountability partner will help them decrease their use and get back on track if they **relapse**. Therapy and twelve-step groups can help the user develop insight into why their habit or addiction developed in the first place (see **defenses, psychological** and **mental health**) and support him in changing his behaviors and when lapses occur. Thus, users need a variety of strategies *in addition* to conscious avoidance of O-Mi's to move on to a healthier life (see **solutions** in the conclusion).

Withdrawal

The combination of physical and mental symptoms that an O-Mi **addict** experiences when they stop porn (or other **drug**) use.

These symptoms include anxiety, guilt, irritability, craving, depression, and restlessness. Porn addicts vary, and not everyone will have the same symptoms (*Sex Addiction Symptoms, Causes and Effects*, n.d.).

Woodsman

Porn industry slang for a man capable of achieving and maintaining an erection, regardless of the situation and without the use of drugs (Reuter, 2004).

The definition given above is from the urbandictionary.com, and perhaps, it is a generally accepted term. The reality is that the definition is an urban myth; male porn actors use various erection-enhancing drugs. Men who act in porn films are expected to easily "get up the wood" (get erections). The pressure is too much for most aspiring male performers, who soon fail out of the business (Faludi, 1999, p. 546).

The required erectile frequency and duration are close to superhuman and beyond the ability of most unassisted men, especially men who are not very young. One veteran male performer reported that "Viagra, Levitra, totally, totally abused. Totally overdosed on. I've heard stories of guys taking three or four pills. They take them like candy" (Grudzen et al., 2009). There are also reports of the use of alprostadil, an injectable drug for those who do not respond to pills. The use of injectables, however, is stigmatized and not allowed by porn film producers (Grudzen et al., 2009; Snow, 2019).

Men who are capable in this area will have longer careers than most female performers, whose faces and bodies quickly cease to be a novelty (see **Coolidge effect**) and who are then replaced by other faces and bodies.

Woodsmen, like female online sex performers, experience emotional **repression**. According to Nina Hartey (Faludi, 1999,

p. 555), "the exploitation of the male" in the porn world "is very distinct in that he must cut off his dick from his heart."

XXX

The label that the porn industry puts on **hard-core** porn films.

XXX is not an official film rating in any country; it is used by the porn industry as an advertising ploy to increase the viewing of their films. These extreme sex films portray **BDSM** and other sexual **fetishes** such as anal sex, **violence against women**, and sex with children (See also **bottom feeder films and TV programs**, **gender inequality**, **kink**, **Pornhub.com**, and **race inequality**). Snuff films that depict killing a woman (or a child) for sexual enjoyment are the most egregious examples. XXX films are now common on online sex sites.

For those who are serious about ending their porn habit, XXX, NC-17, and sexually focused NR films should be blocked on their smart TVs and all other electronic devices.

Conclusion

Banishing the 21st Century <u>PIED</u> Piper; <u>Solutions</u> and Future Directions

Martin Daubney, Dr. John Gottman, Dr. Patrick Carnes, Gary Wilson, and many other experts and commentators have made clear that men's lives are being ruined by pornography use. Their **romantic** partners' lives are being negatively affected as well; they face secrecy, lying, betrayal, and trauma from their boyfriends' or husbands' O-Mi habits, which limit emotional and sexual **intimacy** with their partner. These couples have a good chance of ending up **divorced**. (Daubney, 2017; Gottman, 2016; Smith, 2019; Wilson, 2017). Online sex models and actors also face serious challenges, including multiple health risks and (usually) short careers. It is possible that men with significant O-Mi habits and online porn performers (especially the females) face shorter lives as well, though those statistical determinations have not yet been made.

As sex addiction expert Patrick Carnes (Smith, 2019) notes, the neurobiology of **addiction**, including porn addiction, is becoming "very, very clear." It is a brain disease and can be measured by imaging and through lists of criteria such as those developed by Carnes. Much of the damage done to the brain by porn viewing can, however, be reversed. But helping individuals will not be enough since the **porn pandemic** affects everyone. Many actions will need to be done simultaneously to resolve the issues and **public health** problems created by porn. The ideas below represent many of the suggestions that exist in the literature on O-Mi addiction. While it is undoubtedly not a complete or perfect list, these actions would constitute a good start in addressing the problems that porn is creating.

Litigation is likely to play a significant role in ending the porn pandemic, though efforts on this front are too new to have had a noticeable impact on use. Users just switch to other sites when the stash of porn on one site like **Pornhub.com** is reduced due to legal challenges. **Lawsuits** have been filed against parent companies MindGeek and the WebGroup Czech Republic and their subsidiaries (e.g., Pornhub.com and XVideos.com) for **trafficking** girls and women and selling, publishing, and distributing child porn. Other litigation on behalf of girls and women whose images in pictures and films have been posted without their consent is in progress (*Our Cases*, n.d.). In 2019, twenty-two women received nearly $13 million in a lawsuit against GirlsDoPorn, arguing, among other things, that they were intimidated into performing and that their images were shared online without their agreement. Two years later, the prosecution won a twenty-year sentence against GirlsDoPorn producer Andre Garcias for trafficking women. Though efforts on this front are relatively new, they are likely to increase and limit the amount and type of porn available to consumers (see **legal**).

Jonathan A. Knee, then director of the media program at Columbia Business School, suggested criminalizing "the giving and receiving payment to perform sexual acts, which would make the laws against porn consistent with those of prosti-tution" (Paul, 2005, p.264). In his view, this would avoid the First Amendment issue.

O-Mi websites must be required by law to have a high num-ber of moderators who check a site's pictures and films and keep illegal materials from the site. Not only must the women on the sites be of age (that is, women not girls), they should not be allowed to be made to look like children via makeup or clothing. The law should require large and graphic warnings (for example, a graphic depicting **brain damage**) to be put on the websites, telling those who want to enter that porn use can be addictive and lead to brain injury, depression, memory problems, and **relationship** issues. Independent age verification should be required to enter a site since the neuroplasticity of younger males is greater than that of older males, and they are at risk for abnormal sexual development (Wilson, 2017).

In addition, **obscenity** laws need to be enforced and changed to reflect current circumstances. These laws should target the porn websites that now supply most porn. Awareness that there are such laws and that they are being taken seriously by law enforcement will limit porn production and use. Though individual O-Mi viewers, like individual drug users, would not often be charged, increased awareness of those laws will further stigmatize and discourage use.

While litigation will play a significant role in changing the overall **environment** that supports porn, further steps need to be taken to transform the landscape in which O-Mi viewing occurs. All three aspects of The **triple A engine of porn (AAA: accessibility, anonymity, and affordability**) must be addressed. Programs that block smart TVs, phones, computers, and tablets make porn less **accessible** and should be part of school, work, and other public environments, in addition to being used at home by the recovering user. The CP80 Foundation offers a solution for regulating the internet so that it is easier for users to avoid pornography:

> The proposed plan would divide the Internet into channels, and when a person signs up for Internet service, they could choose to not receive the porn channels if they didn't want them. Those who wish to receive pornographic content would be allowed to do so, thereby not restricting anyone's right to create pornography or consume it, but only allow those who don't wish to have themselves, their families, or their children be exposed to it to have that choice. (Wikipedia Contributors, 2021)

Taxing porn use would make it less affordable (see **johns** and **virtual johns)**. There should be a substantial tax levied on all subscribers to porn sites. Another way to affect the affordability of porn could be life insurance. If future studies show the longevity of those who do a significant amount O-Mi viewing to be less than that of non-porn users, they should pay higher insurance premiums, just as smokers currently do.

Hitting the bottom line of porn purveyors is another strategy for ending the porn pandemic. Credit cards are withdrawing their services from porn sites due to liability concerns related to trafficking and underage girls on the sites. **Boycotting** the products advertised on porn sites will make those sites less attractive to companies and can reduce the profitability of those sites. Social media campaigns in which consumers ask companies to publicly commit to ending their advertising on porn sites have been effective (*Kraft Heinz Pledges*, 2019).

Public health departments and activist organizations should put up billboards depicting the problems created by porn use and making it look "uncool." Some of these billboards should make viewers aware that a trafficking problem is intertwined with porn production.

Culturally, we need to stop winking and thinking, "boys will be boys." "Boys" are capable of emotional growth, of loving their **romantic** partners, and of spiritual development (Chandra, 2012) (see **religion**). **Twelve-step programs**, **accountability partners**, and **therapists** end the anonymity of porn use and can help the user find positive **substitutes** for porn.

Further solutions come from the girlfriends and wives of porn users. A female partner of a porn user who is averse to porn impacting her romantic relationship should practice "**tough love**," not just **love** (see **cheating**, **chipping**, and **divorce**). She should feel free to express anger and dismay over porn use (Heath & Heath, 2010, p. 207) and be clear that she is not willing to accept further O-Mi viewing. Nonporn users looking for a mate should avoid porn users unless they are making significant efforts toward **recovery**. Peer groups and friends who do not view O-Mi's and who are against treating women as **objects** will also be helpful to those trying to quit porn (see **environment**). **Public health** workers should find ways to create ripple effects across social networks, since not only friends but friends' friends and friends' friends' friends may impact O-Mi viewing habits (Christakis & Fowler, 2009, p. 116).

In addition, more education and job opportunities need to be available to young women. An increase in these opportunities would make it possible for many women to leave—or never enter—sex industry work. The poorer **mental health** of some porn models and performers (Mooney, 2019), O-Mi addicts (Wilson, 2017), and the romantic partners of porn users compared to the general population also indicates that psychological services need to be more affordable and available.

Governments should provide funding for exit services that make it possible for women (and men) to leave the porn industry.

Immediate and longer-term help should be available for survivors who want to build a new life. Other countries, including Israel, already do this (Arrow, 2020).

Finally, porn **spam** should not be the backdoor to O-Mi viewing. This spam is not caught by **porn blockers**, but it can cause addiction and **relapse** just like any other porn. The U.K. imposes steep fines on entities that send spam to individuals. Other countries should follow suit.

If porn follows the history of **smoking**, current trends may continue for a long time. Once research showing the negative effects of smoking appeared in 1925 (*1925 Cancer Data*, n.d.), it took many years for governments to begin to discourage smoking and for the environment that promoted smoking to begin to change significantly. A large proportion of the population smoked by the time the problem was widely recognized. Currently, a significant proportion of men view O-Mi's regularly. The problem may get worse before it gets better. One doctor observed that addiction rates could reach fifty percent before we see a reversal (Wilson, 2017, p. 170).

Porn is more insidious than smoking, and its collateral damage to those in the user's life is often invisible. It is viewed in **secret**, and those affected are often unaware or uncertain of how to address what is happening in their lives. It is libido disconnected from care for self, partner (when there is one), and the people on the screen. It parades before us with artificial faces and bodies. Though hidden from sight, its ubiquity indicates that we are a world of hungry, disconnected, and emotionally **repressed** souls. Porn culture is not a happy or healthy culture. We turned the tide on smoking addiction, and we can turn the tide on porn addiction as well.

References

Amen, D. G., & Smith, D. E. (2010). *Unchain your brain: 10 steps to breaking the addictions that steal your life*. MindWorks Press.

Andriote, J. (2018, March 15). You're only as sick as your secrets. *Psychology Today*. **https://www.psychologytoday.com/us/blog/stonewall-strong/201803/youre-only-sick-your-secrets**

Arrow, E. (2020, November 15). The fight for the Nordic Model in Israel with Luba Fein. **https://ellyarrow.wordpress.com/2020/11/15/the-fight-for-the-nordic-model-in-israel-with-luba-fein/**

Bennett, M. (2013, October 9). *The new narcotic*. Public Discourse. **https://www.thepublicdiscourse.com/2013/10/10846/**

Block porn at home on your wifi network using OpenDNS Family shield. (n.d.). Cellphone Safety. **http://www.cellphonesafety.co.za/block-porn-at-home-using-opendns-family-shield.html**

Blythe, A. (n.d.). *4 must-know myths about shame*. BTR. **https://www.btr.org/4-myths-about-shame/**

Bradley, G. (2010). The moral basis for legal regulation of pornography. In James R. Stoner, Jr. & Donna M. Hughes (Eds.), *The Social Costs of Pornography: A Collection of Papers*, (199-217). Witherspoon Institute.

Brassart, S. (2020, November 30). *23 tools for sobriety.* Sex and Relationship Healing. **https://sexandrelationshiphealing.com/blog/23-tools-for-sobriety/**

Braun, L. (2018, January 29). Porn stars seem to be coming, then going: Dying young in the XXX industry. *Toronto Sun.* **https://torontosun.com/entertainment/movies/porn-stars-seem-to-be-coming-then-going-dying-young-in-xxx-industry**

Breastcancer.org Community. (2014). Topic: Is it normal for implants to be cold? [Online forum post]. **https://community.breastcancer.org/forum/44/topics/817685**

Breed, M., & Moore, J. (2016). *Animal Behavior* (2nd ed.). Academic Press.

Bridges, A. J., Wosnitzer, R., Scharrer, E., Sun, C. & Liberman, R. (2010). Aggression and sexual behavior in best selling pornography videos: A content analysis update. *Violence Against Women, 16*(10), 1065–1085. **https://doi.org/10.1177/1077801210382866**

Britannica, Editors of Encyclopaedia (2019, April 15). Jungle fowl. Encyclopedia Britannica. **https://www.britannica.com/animal/jungle-fowl**

Brown Rudnick. (2021, June 17). Brown Rudnick launches landmark case against human trafficking and child pornography in the online porn industry [Press Release]. **https://brownrudnick.com/press_release/brown-rudnick-launches-landmark-case-against-human-trafficking-and-child-pornography-in-the-online-porn-industry/**

Capsular Contracture. (2020, October 29). BreastCancer.org. **https://www.breastcancer.org/treatment/surgery/reconstruction/corrective/capsular-contracture**

Carnes, P. (1983). *Out of the shadows: Understanding sex addiction.* Hazelden Publishing.

Carnes, P. (1991). *Don't call it love: Recovery from sexual addiction.* Bantam.

Casciotti, D., & Zuckerman, D. (n.d.). The benefits of pets for human health. National Center for Health Research. **https://www.center4research.org/benefits-pets-human-health/**

Chandra, R. (2012, January 24). A possible cure for pornography addiction—in an essay. *Psychology Today*. **https://www. psychologytoday.com/us/blog/the-pacific-heart/201201/ possible-cure-pornography-addiction-in-essay**

Christakis, N. A. & Fowler, J. H. (2009). *Connected: The surprising power of our social networks*. Little, Brown and Company.

Cooper, A., Scherer, C. R., Boies, S. C., & Gordon, B. L. (1999) Sexuality on the internet: From sexual exploration to pathological expression. *Professional Psychology: Research and Practice, 30*(2), 154–165. **https://doi.org/10.1037/0735-7028.30.2.154**

Cluster B personality disorder. (n.d.). Family Practice Notebook. **https:// fpnotebook.com/Psych/Behavior/ClstrBPrsnltyDsrdr.htm**

Creighton, S. (2014, April 17). AGAINST: Labiaplasty is an unnecessary cosmetic procedure. *BGOJ: International Journal of Obstetrics and Gynaecology, 121*(6), 768. **(https://obgyn.onlinelibrary.wiley.com/ doi/pdf/10.1111/1471-0528.12620)**

Could religious expectations be the central problem with pornography struggles? (n.d.). Fight the New Drug. **https://fightthenewdrug. org/could-religious-expectations-be-the-central-problem-with- pornography-struggles/**

Daubney, M., (2017, March 29). Men's lives are being ruined by pornography. So why aren't we angry about it? *The Telegraph*. **https://www.telegraph.co.uk/men/thinking-man/ mens-lives-ruined-pornography-arent-angry/**

Davison, M., & Furnham, A. (2018). The personality disorder profile of professional actors. *Psychology of Popular Media Culture, 7*(1), 33-46. **http://dx.doi.org/10.1037/ppm0000101**

de Alarcón, R., de la Iglesia, J. I., Casado, N. M., & Montejo, A. L. (2019). Online porn addiction: What we know and what we don't – A systematic review. *Journal of Clinical Medicine, 8*(1), 91. **https:// doi.org/10.3390/jcm8010091**

Does the porn industry use "tobacco industry tactics" to hide the dark truth? (2018, January 30). Fight the New Drug. **https://fightthenewdrug.org/ porn-industry-uses-tobacco-industry-tactics-to-hide-the-truth/**

Doidge, N. (2007). *The brain that changes itself.* Penguin Books.

Doidge, N. (2013, September 26). Brain scans of porn addicts: What's wrong with this picture? *The Guardian.* **https:// www.theguardian.com/commentisfree/2013/sep/26/ brain-scans-porn-addicts-sexual-tastes**

Eberstadt, M. (2009, April 1). Is pornography the new tobacco? *Policy Review.* **https://www.hoover.org/research/pornography-new-tobacco**

Effects of pornography on marriage. (n.d.). Marripedia. **http://marripedia. org/effects_of_pornography_on_marriage**

Faludi, S. (1999). *Stiffed: The betrayal of the modern man.* Harper Collins.

5 spooky facts about porn that will definitely creep you out. (2020, October 13). Fight the New Drug. **https://fightthenewdrug.org/ spooky-facts-about-porn/**

Folley, A. (2019, January 22). Republican state lawmaker introduces bill that would tax porn to fund Trump's border wall. *The Hill.* **https:// thehill.com/blogs/blog-briefing-room/news/426373-republican- state-lawmaker-introduces-bill-that-would-tax-porn**

Foster, R., Hicks, G., & Seda, J. (2009). *Happiness & health: 9 choices that unlock the powerful connection between the two things we want most.* Tarcher Perigee.

4 triggers that are slipping under your radar. (n.d.). Fortify. **https:// fortifyprogram.tumblr.com/**

Fritz, N., Malic, V., Paul, B., & Zhou, Y. (2020). A descriptive analysis of the types, targets, and relative frequency of aggression in mainstream pornography. *Archives of Sexual Behavior, 49*(8), 3041–3053. **https:// doi.org/10.1007/s10508-020-01773-0**

"Guilt." (n.d.). *Psychology Today.* **https://www.psychologytoday.com/ us/basics/guilt**

Gobry, P. (2019, December 15). *A science-based case for ending the porn epidemic*. EPPC Ethics & Public Policy Center. **https://eppc.org/publication/a-science-based-case-for-ending-the-porn-epidemic/**

Gorski, T. (1989). *The relapse/recovery grid*. Hazelden Publishers.

Gottman, J. & Gottman, J. (2016, April 5). *An open letter on porn*. Gottman.com. **https://www.gottman.com/blog/an-open-letter-on-porn/**

Grey, O. (2019, July 5). *The chilling true story behind the pied piper of Hamlin*. The Portalist. **https://theportalist.com/the-chilling-true-story-behind-the-pied-piper-of-hamelin**

Griffin-Shelley, E., Benjamin, L., & Benjamin, R. (1995). Sex addiction and dissociation. *Sexual Addiction and Compulsivity, 2*(4), 295–306. **https://doi.org/10.1080/10720169508400090**

Grillo, H. (2021, July 2). *What causes people to choose to go into the porn industry?* Fight the New Drug. **https://fightthenewdrug.org/what-causes-people-to-choose-to-go-into-the-porn-industry/**

Grudzen, C. R., Ryan, G., Margold, W., Torres, J., & Gelberg, L. (2009). Pathways to health risk exposure in adult performers. *Journal of Urban Health, 86*(1), 67–78. **https://doi.org/10.1007/s11524-008-9309-4**

Grudzen., C. R., & Kerndt, C. R. (2007). The adult film industry: Time to regulate? *PLoS Medicine, 4*(6): e126. **https://www.medscape.com/viewarticle/560898**

Grudzen, C. R., Meeker, D., Torres, J. M., Du, Q., Morrison, R. S., Andersen, R. M., & Gelberg, L. (2011, June). Comparison of the mental health of female adult performers and other young women in California. *Psychiatric Services, 62*(6), 639–645. **https://ps.psychiatryonline.org/doi/full/10.1176/ps.62.6.pss6206_0639**

Guthrie, C. (n.d.). Why more breast cancer survisors are going flat. *Oprah.com*. **http://www.oprah.com/inspiration/going-flat-why-some-women-reject-breast-reconstruction-surgery**)

Hassed, C. (2017). *The freedom trap: Reclaiming liberty and wellbeing*. Exisle Publishing.

Hassan, A., & Syckle, K. V. (2019, October 13). Porn producers accused of fooling women get sex trafficking charges. *New York Times*. https://www.nytimes.com/2019/10/11/us/porn-sex-trafficking.html

Hatch, L. (2015, December 2). *Four stages of denial of sex addiction*. PsychCentral. https://psychcentral.com/blog/sex-addiction/2015/07/4-stages-of-denial-of-sex-addiction#1

Hawkins, D. (2021, July 16). *Our impact this year—so far!* National Center on Sexual Exploitation. https://endsexualexploitation.org/articles/2021-midyear-impact/

Heath, C., & Heath, D. (2010). *Switch: How to change things when change is hard*. Broadway Books.

Heflick, N. A., & Goldenberg. (2014) Seeing eye to body: The literal objectification of women. *Current Directions in Psychological Science*. https://doi.org/10.1177/0963721414531599

Hess, P. (n.d.). *This is your brain on porn*. Inverse. https://www.inverse.com/article/31799-brain-on-porn-erotica-neuroscience

Hollow, M. C. (2020, June 18). Lessons on coronavirus testing from the adult film industry. *New York Times*. https://www.nytimes.com/2020/06/18/well/live/coronavirus-testing-travel-covid-database-porn-adult-film.html

Hughes, S. M., Aung, T., Harrison, M. A., LaFayette, J. N., & Gallup Jr. G G. (2021). Experimental evidence for sex differences in sexual variety preferences: Support for the Coolidge effect in humans. *Archives of Sexual Behavior, 50*, 495–509. https://doi.org/10.1007/s10508-020-01730-x

Is spamming illegal in the UK? (2020, May 7). EngineMailer. https://www.enginemailer.com/blog/email-marketing-uk-spamming

Kasl, C. D. (1989). *Women, sex, and addiction*. Harper and Row.

Kirkman, M. (2019, March 1). *What do normal labia look like? Sometimes doctors are the wrong people to ask*. Medical Xpress. https://medicalxpress.com/news/2019-03-labia-doctors-wrong-people.html

Kraft Heinz pledges no more porn site ads after NCOSE advocates speak out. (2019, November 7). National Center on Sexual Exploitation. **https://endsexualexploitation.org/articles/kraft-heinz-pledges-no-more-porn-site-ads-after-ncose-advocates-speak-out/**

Kristof, N. (2020, December 4). The children of pornhub. *New York Times.* **https://www.nytimes.com/2020/12/09/opinion/pornhub-news-child-abuse.html**

Layden, M. A. (n.d.). *If pornography made us healthy, we would be healthy by now.* Catholic News Agency. **https://www.catholicnewsagency.com/resource/56077/if-pornography-made-us-healthy-we-would-be-healthy-by-now**

Layden, M. A. (2010). Porn and Violence. In J. R. Stoner & D. M. Hughes (Eds.), *The Social Costs of Pornography: A Collection of Papers* (57–68). Witherspoon Institute.

Lehmiller, J. J. (2017, August 3). How much gender inequality is there in internet pornography? *Psychology Today.* **https://www.psychologytoday.com/us/blog/the-myths-sex/201708/how-much-gender-inequality-is-there-in-internet-pornography**

Littlejohn, D. (2009). *The 12-step Buddhist.* Atria Books.

Love, I. (2016, December 21). *Full spectrum bliss: The secret to an oxytocin based sexual connection.* Before It's News. **https://beforeitsnews.com/alternative/2016/12/full-spectrum-bliss-the-secret-to-an-oxytocin-based-sexual-connection-3454642.html**

Love, T., Laier, C., Brand, M., Hatch. L., & Hajela, R. (2015). Neuroscience of internet pornography addiction: A review and update. *Behavioral Sciences, 5*(3), 388–433. **https://doi.org/10.3390/bs5030388**

Madison, H., (2015). *Down the rabbit hole: Curious adventures and cautionary tales of a former Playboy bunny.* HarperCollins.

Maltz, W., & Maltz, L. (2008). *The porn trap: The essential guide to overcoming problems caused by pornography.* Harper Collins.

Maren, J. V. (2019, January 7). *Many porn stars viewed online are actually dead and buried... their 'work' killed them* [blog post]." The Bridgehead. **https://thebridgehead.ca/2019/01/07/many-porn-stars-viewed-online-are-actually-dead-and-buriedtheir-work-killed-them/**

Maren, J. V. (2020, April 20). *Rise in young men bored by mainstream pornography turning to child sex-abuse for kicks* [blog post]. LifeSite. **https://www.lifesitenews.com/blogs/rise-in-young-men-bored-by-mainstream-pornography-turning-to-child-sex-abuse-for-kicks**

Marriage and men's health. (2019, June 5). Harvard Health Publishing. **https://www.health.harvard.edu/mens-health/marriage-and-mens-health**

Meyers, J. (2017, Decembr 7). China's 'sexy cyborg' took on Silicon Valley bro culture – and won. *Los Angeles Times.* **https://www.latimes.com/world/asia/la-fg-china-sexy-cyborg-2017-story.html**

Mickelwait, L. (2021, February 13). The end of Pornhub's campaign of intimidation. *Washington Examiner.* **https://www.washingtonexaminer.com/opinion/op-eds/the-end-of-pornhubs-campaign-of-intimidation**

Miller, B. (2018). *Airplane passenger caught reading porn in-flight.* National Center on Sexual Exploitation. **https://endsexualexploitation.org/articles/reading-porn-manga/**

Milos, R. (2019, November 4). *Control your inner critic and stop your stinkin thinkin.* Rehab.com. **https://rehabs.com/pro-talk/control-your-inner-critic-and-stop-your-stinkin-thinkin/**

Mooney, T. (2019, December 6). *Adult film performers say the state of mental health in the industry needs more attention.* CBS News. **https://www.cbsnews.com/news/adult-film-performers-say-the-state-of-mental-health-in-the-industry-needs-more-attention/**

More sex addiction treatment resources. (n.d.). Hope & Freedom. **https://www.hopeandfreedom.com/more-treatment-resources**

Neef, N. D., Coppens, V., Huys, W., & Morrens, M. (2019). Bondage-Discipline, dominance-submission and sadomasochism (BDSM) from an integrative biopsychosocial perspective: A systematic review. *Sexual medicine, 7*(2), 129–144. **https://doi.org/10.1016/j.esxm.2019.02.002**

Newman, A. (2017, February 10). *"No one warned her": The unexpected effects of breast reconstruction.* Our Bodies Our Selves. **https://www.ourbodiesourselves.org/2017/02/the-unexpected-effects-of-breast-reconstruction/**

1925 Cancer Data. (n.d.). The Crime Prevention Group. **https://www.members.tripod.com/medicolegal/cancerstats1925.htm**

Our cases. (n.d.). National Center on Sexual Exploitation. **https://sexualexploitationlawsuits.com/our-cases/**

Oss, M. V. (2020, September 30). *Law center files first ever anti-trafficking lawsuit against pornography producers on behalf of survivor.* DrRichSwier.com. NCOSE. **https://drrichswier.com/2020/09/30/law-center-files-first-ever-anti-trafficking-lawsuit-against-pornography-producers-on-behalf-of-survivor/**

Pappas, S. (2012, May 31). *Men's porn use linked to unhappy relationships.* Live Science. **https://www.livescience.com/20684-porn-relationships.html**

Paul, P. (2005). *Pornified: How pornography is transforming our lives, our relationships, and our families.* Times Books.

Pearsall, P. (1994). *A healing intimacy: The power of loving connections.* Random House.

Peele, S. (2004). *7 tools to beat addiction: A new path to recovery from addictions of any kind: Smoking, alcohol, food, drugs, gambling, sex, love.* Three Rivers Press.

Peele, S. (2015, April 11). *12 concepts of recovery that have stood the test of time.* The Fix. **https://www.thefix.com/content/12-ways-overcome-your-or-others-addictions**

Perry, S. L., & Schleifer, C. (2017). Till porn do us part? A longitudinal examination of pornography use and divorce. *Journal of Sex Research, 55*(3), 284–296. **https://doi.org/10.1080/00224499.2017.1317709**

Porter, S. (2020, October 26). Study shows porn profits from and promotes racism. *The Washington Examiner.* **https://www.washingtonexaminer.com/opinion/op-eds/study-shows-porn-profits-from-and-promotes-racism**

Psychology Today Staff. (n.d.). Dopamine. *Psychology Today.* **https://www.psychologytoday.com/us/basics/dopamine**

Reese, H. (2019). *Don't fear the sex recession.* JStor Daily. **https://daily.jstor.org/dont-fear-sex-recession/**

Regnerus, M., & Uecker, J. (2011). *Premarital sex in America: How young Americans meet, mate, and think about marrying.* Oxford University Press.

Reuter, P. (2004, February 2). *Woodsman.* **https://www.urbandictionary.com/define.php?term=woodsman**

Richters, J., de Visser, R. O., Rissel, C. E. Grulich, A. E., & Smith, A. M. (2008). Demographic and psychosocial features of participants in bondage and discipline, "sadomasochism" or dominance and submission (BDSM): Data from a national survey. *The Journal of Sexual Medicine, 5*(7), 1660–1668. **https://doi.org/10.1111/j.1743-6109.2008.00795.x**

Roizen, M. (2004). *The real age makeover.* Harper Collins.

Rubin, G. (2015). *Better than before: Mastering the habits of our everyday lives.* Crown Publishers.

Sex addiction symptoms, causes and effects. (n.d.). PsychGuides.com. **https://www.psychguides.com/behavioral-disorders/sex-addiction/**

Shea, S. (2015, September 9). This is your brain on porn. *Philadelphia Inquirer.* **https://www.inquirer.com/philly/news/20150909_This_is_your_brain_on_porn.html**

Short., M. B., Kasper, T. E., & Wetterneck, C. (2014). The relationship between religiosity and internet pornography use. *Journal of Religion and Health, 54*(2), 571–583. **10.1007/s10943-014-9849-8**

Silverstein, J. (2018, July 17). Q & A: *Compulsive sexual behavior disorder added to ICD-11 as mental disorder.* Healio. **https://www.healio. com/news/psychiatry/20180717/qa-compulsive-sexual-behavior-disorder-added-to-icd11-as-mental-disorder**

Smith, L., & Vardaman, S. H. (2010). The problem of demand in combating sex trafficking. *Revue Internationale de Droit Pénal, 81*(3), 607. **https://doi.org/10.3917/ridp.813.0607**

Smith, T. (2019). Recovery & treament of sexual addiction: An interview with Dr. Patrick Carnes. *Open Access Journal of Addiction and Psychology, 2*(5). **https://irispublishers.com/oajap/pdf/OAJAP. MS.ID.000549.pdf**

Snow, A., (2019, August 3). Exposing male porn stars' dirty little secret: 'Do you want to pop a pill?' **https://www.thedailybeast.com/ exposing-male-porn-stars-dirty-little-secret-do-you-want-to-pop-a-pill?ref=scroll**

St. James, I. (2006). *Bunny tales: Behind closed doors at the Playboy Mansion.* Running Press Book Publishers.

Stansvik, F. (2018). Keeping love at a distance: An interpretative phenomenological analysis of former pornography addicts' experiences with pornography. [Masters thesis.] University of Gothenburg. **https://gupea.ub.gu.se/bitstream/2077/58738/1/ gupea_2077_58738_1.pdf**

STATEMENT: *GirlsDoPorn producer rightly sentenced to twenty years for sex trafficking.* (2021, June 15). National Center on Sexual Exploitation. **https://endsexualexploitation.org/articles/ statement-girlsdoporn-producer-rightly-sentenced-to-20-years-for-sex-trafficking/**

Stevenson, R. L. (1968). *Dr. Jekyll and Mr. Hyde and other stories.* Lancer Books.

Strand, P. (2021, February 24). *2021 'Dirty dozen list' says internet giants like Amazon, Netflix and Reddit fueling sexual exploitation.* CBNNews. **https://www1.cbn.com/cbnnews/us/2021/february/2021-dirty-dozen-list-says-internet-giants-like-amazon-netflix-and-reddit-fueling-sexual-exploitation**

The Supreme Court defines obscenity. (n.d.). Encyclopedia.com. **https://www.encyclopedia.com/law/legal-and-political-magazines/supreme-court-defines-obscenity**

Taube, A. (2013, October 7). *Lured by heavy web traffic, mainstream brands are running ads on adult sites.* Insider. **https://www.businessinsider.com/don-jon-advertises-on-adult-site-pornhub-2013-10**

Than, K., & Taylor, A. P. (2021, May 17). *What is Darwin's theory of evolution?* LiveScience. https://www.livescience.com/474-controversy-evolution-works.html

Thompson, D., (2019, October 20). *Tying the knot is tied to longer life span, new data shows.* WebMd. **https://www.webmd.com/a-to-z-guides/news/20191010/marriage-tied-to-longer-life-span-new-data-shows**

Tokyo University of Science. (2020, July 20). 'Love hormone' oxytocin could be used to treat cognitive disorders like Alzheimer's. *ScienceDaily.* **www.sciencedaily.com/releases/2020/07/200720093308.htm**

Trafficking Hub. (n.d.). Shutdown pornhub and hold its executives accountable for aiding trafficking [change.org petition]. **https://traffickinghubpetition.com/**

Trueman, P. A., & Rogers, G. (2019, December 24). Pornography consumption: The overlooked public health crisis. *The Hill.* **https://thehill.com/opinion/healthcare/475806-pornography-consumption-the-overlooked-public-health-crisis**

Twenge, J. M. (2017). *iGen: Why today's super-connected kids are growing up less rebellious, more tolerant, less happy—and completely unprepared for adulthood—and what that means for the rest of us.* Atria Books.

Vaillant, G. (2012). *Triumphs of Experience: The men of the Harvard grant study*. The Belknap Press.

Volkow, N. D, Koob, G. F., & McLellan. (2016). Neurobiologic advances from the brain disease model of addiction. *New England Journal of Medicine, 374,* 363-371. **https://www.nejm.org/doi/full/10.1056/NEJMra1511480**

Watching pornography rewires the brain to a more juvenile state. (2019, December 29). NeuroscienceNews.com. **https://neurosciencenews.com/neuroscience-pornography-brain-15354/**

Weaver, J. B., 3rd, Weaver, S. S., Mays, D., Hopkins, G. L., Kannenberg, W., & McBride, D. (2011). Mental- and physical-health indicators and sexually explicit media use behavior by adults. *The Journal of Sexual Medicine, 8*(3), 764–772. **https://doi.org/10.1111/j.1743-6109.2010.02030.x**

Weiss, R. (2013, February 27). Addiction and narcissistic shame. PsychCentral. **https://psychcentral.com/blog/sex/2013/02/addiction-narcissistic-shame#1**

Wikipedia contributors. (2021, June 23). The CP80 Foundation. In *Wikipedia, The Free Encyclopedia.* Retrieved September 4, 2021, from **https://en.wikipedia.org/w/index.php?title=The_CP80_Foundation&oldid=1030077501**

Wilcox, W. B. & Stone, L. (2019, April 4). The happiness recession. *The Atlantic.* **https://www.theatlantic.com/ideas/archive/2019/04/happiness-recession-causing-sex-depression/586405/**

Wilson, G. (2017). *Your brain on porn: Internet pornography and the emerging science of addiction* (Rev. ed.). Commonwealth Publishing.

Wood, W., (2019). *Good habits, bad habits: The science of making positive changes that stick.* Farrar, Straus and Gireaux.

Wolters Kluwer Health. (2018, September 17). Silicone breast implants linked to increased risk of some rare harms: First comprehensive study of long-term outcomes in 'postapproval' database. *ScienceDaily.* **www.sciencedaily.com/releases/2018/09/180917191649.htm**

Zakaria, R. (2010, May 19). Female genital mutilation vs. female breast mutilation. *Ms.* **Female Genital Mutilation vs. Female Breast Mutilation - Ms. Magazine (msmagazine.com)**

www.ingramcontent.com/pod-product-compliance
Lightning Source LLC
Chambersburg PA
CBHW060238030426
42335CB00014B/1510